THE COMMUNES OF LOMBARDY
FROM THE VI. TO THE X. CENTURY

LECTOR HOUSE PUBLIC DOMAIN WORKS

THE COMMUNES OF LOMBARDY FROM THE VI. TO THE X. CENTURY

WILLIAM KLAPP WILLIAMS,
HERBERT B. ADAMS

ISBN: 978-93-5614-476-7

Published: 1891

LECTOR HOUSE

LECTOR HOUSE LLP
E-MAIL: lectorpublishing@gmail.com

JOHNS HOPKINS UNIVERSITY STUDIES IN HISTORICAL AND POLITICAL SCIENCE

HERBERT B. ADAMS, EDITOR

History is past Politics and Politics present History.—*Freeman*

NINTH SERIES

V-VI

THE COMMUNES OF LOMBARDY FROM THE VI. TO THE X. CENTURY

AN INVESTIGATION OF THE CAUSES WHICH LED TO THE DEVELOPMENT OF MUNICIPAL UNITY AMONG THE LOMBARD COMMUNES

BY

WILLIAM KLAPP WILLIAMS, PH.D.

NEWBERRY LIBRARY, CHICAGO

1891

"Est error spretus, quo Langobarda juventus
Errabat, verum loquitur nunc pagina sensum."

Rhotari: Legum Prologus.

CONTENTS

THE COMMUNES OF LOMBARDY FROM THE VI. TO THE X. CENTURY.

PART I.

THE LOMBARD CONQUEST AND ITS RESULTS.

Before tracing the beginnings of renewed municipal life in Northern Italy, we must consider the conditions of land and people, which first rendered possible and then fostered the spirit of local independence of which such beginnings were the natural expression. To do this we must commence our researches with the first domination of the Lombards in the country.

In detail the story of the conquest of Northern Italy by the Lombards under Alboin, in 568, hardly differs materially from that of the inroads of other barbarian tribes of the north on the fertile plains of Italy. The causes were the same. Where the distinction is to be found from other such invasions, is in the results of the Lombard occupation, and in the different methods which the Lombards adopted so as to render their power and their possessions permanent. Let us look at the character of this invading host, which sweeps like a tide, at once destroying and revivifying, over the exhausted though still fertile plains of the Po and the Adige. Are we to call it a moving people or an advancing army? Are we to call its leaders (*duces*, from *ducere* to lead), heads of clans and families, or captains and generals? Finally, is the land to be invaded, or is the land to be settled? To all these questions the only answer is to be found in the conception of the absolute union of both the kinds of functions described. A people is moving from a home whose borders have proved too narrow for its increasing numbers; an army is conquering a new home, where plenty will take the place of want, and luxury of privation. It is not an army marching at the command of a strongly centralized power to conquer a rich neighbor, and force a defeated enemy to pay it service or tribute. It is a body which, when it has conquered as an army, will occupy as a people; when it is established as a people, will still remain an army. The sword was not turned into the ploughshare; but the power to wield the sword had given the right to till the land, and soon the power to hold the land was to give the right to wear the sword. It was the conquest of a highly civilized agricultural people—whose very civilization had reduced them to a stage of moral weakness which rendered them totally unfit to defend themselves—by a semi-barbarous people, agricultural also, but rude, uncivilized, independent, owning no rulers but their family or military chiefs.

The conquerors took possession of the country simply as they would take possession of a larger farm than they had before owned. Their riches were only such as served for the support of men—herds, land, wine and corn. They needed cultivators for their large farm, so instead of destroying every one with fire and sword, they spared those of the weak inhabitants of the land who had survived the first onslaught, in order that they might make use of farmers to cultivate their new possessions. In most cases they did not make slaves of them, but tributaries; and after the land had been portioned evenly among the soldiers of the invading host, the original holders of the land tilled it themselves, under a system somewhat kindred to the metayer system as to-day existent in Tuscany and elsewhere, paying, according to the usual custom adopted by the northern conquerors of Italy, one-third of the produce[1] to their new masters. The whole organization of society was on a purely military basis; the soldiers of the conquering army, although they became landed proprietors, none the less retained their character and name of soldiers. Hence when these crude forms of social life began to crystallize into the carefully marked ranks of the feudal system, the *"milites"*[2] formed the order of gentlemen, the smaller feudatories, who gave land in fief to their vassals—generally the old inhabitants—while holding their own nominally from the *"duces,"* or dukes, the representatives of their former leaders in war, who held their tenure direct from the king or chief.

As the object of this paper is particularly to trace the origin and early sources of municipal life in Northern Italy, let us turn and see what were the effects on the already existing towns, of the inroads of these hordes of northern barbarians. At the outset I must state emphatically that all our sources of information as to the institutional history of this obscure period are exceedingly vague, meagre and unsatisfactory. The progress of events we can follow with more or less accuracy from the mazy writings of the early chroniclers; we can get a fair idea of the judicial and the legislative acts of the ruling powers by studying and comparing the different codes of laws that have come down to us; but in a study of the internal municipal life of these early ages, the student meets again and again with increasing discouragement, and soon finds himself almost hopelessly lost in a tangle of doubts and inferences.

In the almost total want of direct evidence, from casual mention gleaned from the writings of the chroniclers, and from occasional references in the law codes to municipal offices and regulations, enough indirect evidence must be sought, to enable us, by the aid of our powers of reasoning, if not of our imagination, to build up some history, defective though it be, of municipal life, down to the time when the internal growth and importance of the cities rendered them sufficiently prominent political factors to have their deeds and their progress chronicled. Besides, if we consider the modes by which the communes slowly rose to independence, it

---

[1] *Paulus Diaconus*: De Gest. Lang., Lib. II., c. 32. v. *Muratori*: Script. Rer. Ital., T. I., p. 436. The Gothic system was to take one-third of the land itself from the conquered people; the Lombards on the other hand took one-third of the produce, *"frugum."*

[2] With the growth of society and the increase of population, the *milites* gain added power, and become the *"catanei,"* the barons of the period, or as some are pleased to call them, the *"rural counts."*

will easily be seen that to have every step of this slow and almost secret advance chronicled and given to the world, would have been entirely contrary to the policy of the cities. These hoped to gain by the neglect of their rulers, and while clinging pertinaciously to every privilege ever legally granted, to claim new ones constantly, putting forth as their sole legal title that slippery claim of precedent and time-honored custom. In that age, books of reference to prove such claims would have been found alike inconvenient and unnecessary. All the city folks wished was to be forgotten and ignored by their superiors, as any notice vouchsafed them was sure to come only in the restraint of some assumed privilege or the curtailing of some coveted right.

Hence the principal cause of the poverty of record through all this period of slow if steady growth; and the disappointed investigator must in some measure console himself with such a reason. It may be asked, what of the various local histories of different towns, whose authors seldom fail to give highflown accounts of their native cities, even in the remotest and darkest ages of their history? To this question there is a double answer: in the first place the uttermost caution must be enjoined in using such material; not only in separating fact from baseless tradition of a much later period, but in making large allowance for the heavy strain which a strong feeling of local patriotism, or civism, puts upon the conscience of the author. In the second place it must be remembered that most of such histories, or at least of the monkish or other records from which they derive their source and most of their material, were written to the glory or under the auspices of some dominant noble family or ecclesiastical institution, to whose laudation in ages past and present the humble author devotes all the resources of his mind, and I am afraid far too often of his imagination.

Let us now cast a glance at the exhausted civilization of the towns of Northern Italy, where the formal shell of Roman organization still remained, after the vigor and life which had produced it had long been destroyed. To describe the condition of the Roman *municipia* at the time of the Teutonic invasions is but to tell a part of the story of the fall of the Roman Empire. The municipal system, which from the names and duties of its officers would seem to represent a surprising amount of local independence in matters of administration, even a collection of small almost free republics, had lost all its strength and all its vital power by the grinding exactions of a centralized despotism, which was compelled to support its declining power by strengthening the very forces which were working its destruction, at the expense of destroying those from which it should have gained its strength. The stability of every state rests ultimately on the wealth and character of its citizens, and any government which exhausts the one and degrades the other in an effort to maintain its own unlimited power has its days numbered. Under the despotic rule of the later emperors the municipalities had lost all their power, though in theory their rights were unassailed. The *curia* could elect its magistrates as of old, and these magistrates could legislate for the *municipium*, but by a single word the imperial delegate could annul the choice of the one and the acts of the other.

The economic condition of the people amounted to little short of bankruptcy; the possession of wealth, in landed property especially, having become but a burden to be avoided, and a source of exaction rather than of satisfaction to the owner. The inequalities of burdens and of rank were great. The citizens were divided into three classes: (1) the privileged classes, (2) the Curials, (3) the common people. The first, freely speaking, were those who had in a manner succeeded in detaching themselves from the interests of the *municipium* to which they belonged; such were the members of the Senate, including all with the indefinite title of *clarissimi*, the soldiers, the clergy, the public magistrates as distinguished from the municipal officers. The second consisted of all citizens of a town, whether natives—*municipes*—or settlers—*incolae*—who possessed landed property of more than twenty-five *jugera*, and did not belong to any privileged class: both these classes were hereditary. The third, of all free citizens whose poverty debarred them from belonging to either of the preceding divisions. On the second of these classes, the Curials, fell all the grinding burdens of the state, the executing of municipal duties, and the exactions of the central government.

It is not necessary for me to trace here the development of that financial policy which resulted in the ruin, I may say the annihilation of this order. Suffice it to say that it formed the capital fund of the government which exhausted it, and when the source of supply was destroyed, production ceased, and with it, of course, all means of governmental support. Where the extinction of this "middle class" touches the point of our inquiry is in affording an explanation of a circumstance in the history of the Lombard subjugation of the Italian towns, which without consideration of this fact would appear almost incomprehensible. I refer to the utter passivity of the inhabitants, not only in the matter of resistance to attack, which the greater strength and courage of the invaders perhaps rendered useless, but in what is more surprising, the fact that after the easy conquest was completed, we hear nothing of the manner in which the people adapted themselves to the totally new condition of life and of government to which they were subjected. Even if we can understand hearing nothing of what the people did, at least we should expect to hear what was done with it, what it became. The story of its resistance might be short and soon forgotten, but the story of its sufferings, of its complaints, of struggle against the entire change in the order and character of its life, should be a long one.

But of this no record, hardly mention even appears. When the central government falls and the last of its legions are destroyed or have departed, there seems to be no thought of any other element in society. If the evidence of the law codes did not tell us that a Roman population existed, history would record little to indicate its presence. Not only is even the slightest trace of nationality effaced, but the merging of the old conditions of life into the new seems of too little consequence to merit even an allusion. This state of affairs, as said above, is caused by the annihilation, by the despotic power of the central government, of that middle class which in times of prosperity formed the sinews of the state. Of the other classes, the privileged class, with the exception of the clergy, fell of course with the government which supported it, and the common people possessed no individuality, no power, and hardly any rights. Such, then, was the condition of the towns at the time of the Lombard invasion, a condition of such abasement and such degradation as literally to have no history; a condition which indeed can truthfully be said to merit none.

History tells the story of every great nation on the face of the earth in three short words, growth, supremacy, decline. Vary the theme as you may in the countless histories of countless peoples; subdivide the course of its progress as you will, allowing for different local causes and different local phenomena, the true philosophy of history teaches that no real departure from this natural development is possible. But what if by the violent intervention of some new and entirely foreign force, another development and another life is given to the inanimate ashes of the old? What if some nation, fresh from the woods and fields of the childhood of its growth, come with overwhelming yet preserving strength and infuse new blood into the withered veins of its predecessor? This is the problem we now have before us. How many writers of Italian history have entitled this chapter in its development "A new Italian Nation formed"! It is not the old glories of Rome, which had been Italy, returning; it is a new Italian nation formed. Each word tells a story of its own. It is not the old galvanized to a second life; it is the new superimposed, violently if you will, upon it. We do not hear of Athens or of Rome, of an Alexander or of a Caesar, of a city or of a man. It is an "Italian nation." It is the individualism of the independent spirit of the North, which "forms" a nation from the exhausted remains of the development of centralization of the South. The new idea of distinct nationality among races of kindred stock was already at work, even though it did not reach a formal expression till the Treaty of Verdun, more than two hundred and fifty years later.

I do not mean to imply that we must in any measure ignore the passive force and influence of the old forms on the new. The old veins receive the new blood; the new torrent, overrunning everything at first with the strength of its new life, will find again, even if it deepen, the channel of the old river: a vanquished civilization will always subdue and at the same time raise its barbarous conquerors, if they come of a stock capable of appreciating civilizing influences. In the present case this means that the men of the North brought the new ideas that were to form modern history, and let their growth be directed and assisted, while they were yet too young to stand alone, by some of the framework which had been built up by the long experience of their Southern neighbors.

To focus this thought on the immediate subject of our present study, this I think is the only and true solution of the tedious question, so much discussed by the two opposing schools of thought: whether the government of the Italian communes was purely Roman in its forms and in its conception, or purely Teutonic. The supporters of neither theory can be said to be in the right. You cannot say that the average city government was entirely Roman or entirely Teutonic, either in the laws which guided it, or in the channels by which these laws were executed and expressed. I think much time and much learning have been spent on a discussion both fruitless and unnecessary. We cannot err if we subject the question to a consideration at once critical and impartial.

The widely differing opinions eagerly supported by different writers on this point, form a very good example of the deceiving influence of national feeling on the judgment in matters of historical criticism. For, on the one hand, we find many German writers ignoring entirely the old framework of Roman organization, and recognizing only the new Teutonic life which gave back to it the strength it had lost; on the other, a host of lesser Italian writers who magnify certain old names and forms, and mistake them for the substance, making all the new life of Italy but the return of a past, which belonged to a greatness that was dead. Many there are of this school in Italy, where you will often find to-day a commune of three hundred inhabitants, with its one or two constables wearing the imperial badge, "*Senatus Populusque Albanensis*" or "*Verulensis,*" as the case may be. Truly a suggestive anachronism! It is true that in remote ages especially, when the records of history are few and uncertain—and the period we are considering in this paper can almost be called the prehistoric age of municipal institutions in Northern Italy—much can be learned and much truth inferred from the evidence of a name. But this is a species of evidence we can never be too cautious in using, as the temptation is always to infer too much rather than too little.

In the following pages I will try to sift the evidence obtainable, with the impartiality of one trammeled by the support of no particular theory; always bearing in mind, however, one fact, all-important in a study where so much depends on nomenclature, namely, to give that shade of meaning and that amount of weight to any term which it possessed in the age in which it was used, carefully distinguishing this from its use in any earlier or later age. The importance of this caution will be soon seen when we come to discuss the origin of corporate life in the communes, where many have been misled by attaching to the words *respublica* and *civitas*, for example, so continually recurring in the old laws and charters, a meaning which was entirely foreign to the terms at the period of their use. With this warning, we will turn to a consideration of the first effects of the inroad of the northern barbarians on the cities, whose exhausted and defenseless state has already been pointed out.

One of the chief characteristics of the Teutonic tribes which overran Italy during the fifth and sixth centuries, was an innate hatred of cities, of enclosing walls and crowded habitations. Children of the field and the forest, they had their village communities and their hundreds, their common land and their allotted land, but these were small restrictions on their free life, and left an extended "airspace" for each individual and his immediate household. Homestead was not too near homestead, each man being separated from his neighbor by the extent of half the land belonging to each. The centralization of population in city life was a thing undreamed of, and an idea abhorred, alike for its novelty and for the violence it did to the as yet untrained instincts of the people. The strong, independent individualism of the Teutonic freeman rebelled against anything which would in any way limit his freedom of action: "ne pati quidem inter se junctas sedes," says Tacitus.[3] An agriculturist in his rude way, he lived on the land which supported him and his family, and feeling no further need, his untrained intelligence could form no conception of the necessities and the advantages of the social union and interdependence of a more civilized state of society; nor could he comprehend the

---

[3] *Tacitus*: Germania, cap. xvi.

mutual relations of the individual to the immediate community in which he lived.

He could understand his own relation to and dependence on the state as a whole; alone he could not repel the attacks of neighboring tribes, alone he could not go forth to conquer new lands or increase the number of his herds. But why he should associate with others and so limit the freedom which was his birthright, for other purposes than those of attack and defense, of electing a leader for war, or getting his allotment of land in peace, was altogether beyond the horizon of his comprehension. He was sufficient unto himself for all the purposes of his daily life; to the product of his own plough and hunting-spear he looked for the maintenance of himself and his family, and the loose organization which we may call the state existed simply so as to enable him to live in comparative peace, or gain advantage in war—perhaps the first example of the new power in state-craft which was to revolutionize the political principles of the world; the individual lived no longer simply to support the state, but the state existed solely to protect and aid the individual.

If all this be true of the Teutonic nations in general, in the earlier stages of their development, particularly true is it of the Lombards,[4] a wild tribe of the Suevic stock, whose few appearances in history, previous to their invasion of Italy, are connected only with the fiercest strife and the rudest forms of barbarism. History seems to have proved that tradition has maligned the Vandal; the Goth can boast a ruler raised at the centre of Eastern civilization and refinement; but the Lombard of the invasion can never appear as other than the rude barbarian rushing from his wild northern home, and forcing on a defenseless people the laws and the customs suited to his own rugged nature and the unformed state of society in which he lived.

Such being the case, there is little cause for wonder that the invading Lombard directed his fury with particular violence against the corporate towns, whose strength was not sufficient to resist the attacks of his invading host. Like all other Teutonic tribes the Lombards were entirely unskilled in the art of attacking fortified towns; hence the only mode of siege with which they were acquainted was that of starving out the inhabitants, by cutting off all source of supply by ravaging and destroying the surrounding country. This fact, unimportant as it may seem at the first glance, materially affected the whole course of the later history of some of the Italian cities. By this means we are enabled, even at this early epoch, to divide them into two classes. First, those cities which, after a more or less short resistance,

---

[4] The Sagas say the Lombards came originally from Scandinavia. Their name is commonly derived from "Long-beard," but more probably came from words signifying "a long stretch of land." Their first appearance in history is during the first century of the Christian era, in the region of Magdeburg. All trace of them is then lost till they reappear in the fifth century on the banks of the Oder; they then go south to the river Theiss. They are in a constant state of war with the Gepidae, a tribe nearly as fierce as themselves, which strife is supposed to have been fomented by the eastern emperors. In the year 567 the Lombards, under their king Alboin, together with the Avars, begin to move into Pannonia from Dacia and the region of the Don. Kunnemund, the king of the Gepidae, is killed, and his conquered people merged in the race of their conquerors. In the next year, still victorious, they overrun Northern Italy.

yielded to the rude tactics of the barbarians and were made subject by them, for example Milan and Pavia.[5] Second, those cities like Venice and Ravenna,[6] which, by means of a connection with the sea which the invaders could not cut off, were enabled to gain supplies by water, and so resist all efforts of the besieging host to capture them. They never fell completely under the Lombard yoke, and either retained a sort of partial autonomy or yielded allegiance to some other power. It is the cities of the former class that are the subject of this investigation.

The condition of these inland towns at the time of the invasion was, as we have seen, weak in the extreme. The defenses, where they existed, were of a character to afford little protection, and the bulk of the inhabitants were so enervated from a life of poverty and oppression that they were almost incapable of offering any resistance in their own defense. They were reduced to such a condition as to be only too grateful if their rough conquerors, after an easy victory, disdainfully spared their lives, and left them to occupy their dismantled dwellings.

This seems to have been the almost universal method of procedure. The Lombards did not in any sense, at first, think of occupying the conquered cities; for the reasons already given they despised, because they could not yet comprehend, the life of the civilian. They contented themselves with pulling down the walls, razing the fortifications, and destroying every mark which would make of the city anything but an aggregate of miserable dwellings. The inhabitants were for the most part spared, and left to enjoy, if the term can be used for such an existence, what the conquerors did not think worth the having. These felt the fruits of their victory to lie in the rich arable lands of the surrounding plains, and here they settled down, each in his own holding, portioned out by lot to every soldier; the town being considered but as a part of the *civitas* or district, if I may use the term, of the *dux* or overlord, from whom the several *milites*, or landholders of the surrounding territory, had their tenure, and who himself held directly from the king.

It is the very insignificance of the municipal unit at this time that makes it so difficult to determine anything accurate of its position. It existed, but little more can be said of it; indeed, even this statement might be questioned, if we make that term signify a corporate existence, as will be seen further on when we come to discuss the question of the unbroken corporate existence of the towns. In a feudal age, or in an age of incipient feudalism, obligation, either claimed from an inferior or yielded to a superior, is a good index of rank and importance. Until we find the cities fulfilling certain obligations required by a higher power, we can learn little to tell of their condition or of their internal history. On the other hand, when we find the time come for fulfilling certain obligations, we can safely argue that the cities have acquired certain functions which put them in a position to meet the obligations which their growing importance has caused to be exacted of them. To trace these steps accurately and satisfactorily is impossible, but by the aid of collateral evidence a rough idea of the epochs at least of their progress can be gained.

[5] Some of these cities were enabled to hold out for a considerable period. Pavia was not taken till 572.

[6] To these seaports some of the functionaries of the inland towns, especially among the clergy, were able to effect their escape. For instance, the Archbishop of Milan fled to Genoa, and the Archbishop of Aquileja to Venice.

For this first period, then, we see the towns reduced to the lowest depths of wretchedness and disintegration; critically speaking hardly existing, but simply holding together. In studying institutions and tracing the course of their development, we must always remember that the uninterrupted continuance of their history may depend as much on the moral force of their existence as on the more limited and defined fact of their accurate and legal recognition by others. In every society a state of fact must in time become a state of law, as wise legislation is more the recognition by law of existing conditions than the formulating of new codes. So the towns, even at the period immediately succeeding their conquest by the Lombards, though their corporate existence cannot be claimed, nevertheless cannot be said in any measure to have ceased to exist; for as collections of individuals and of dwellings they were there, with an individuality uneffaced though as yet unrecognized.

It was a period of utter stagnation, of suspension of life, but the source remained intact, from which, by the evolution of events and the progress of time, seeds were to spring that only needed external pressure to force them into a growth, slow indeed but certain, and in the end fruitful. A transition period we might call it. The theory of Roman universal domination, by relegating to the central power all the *political* functions of the municipality and leaving it only its *civic* ones, and these in later imperial times grudgingly and with an impaired independence, had left it simply an administrative instead of a political division of the state. In the flush of triumph the rough hand of the barbarian overthrew the framework of administration, and at first failed to recognize the necessity of replacing it by any other. The passivity of the conquered inhabitants—the cause of which has already been explained—was such that a long period elapsed before they realized that to regain in some measure the position of local independence that they had lost, and to free themselves from the shackles of dependence on the rural communities in which they were placed—a dependence forced upon them by the natural development of the new state system of their Teutonic conquerors—some common effort at organization was needful, for purposes at least of self-defense. That this effort came from the town itself, from the people and not from the external power of the ruler or overlord, is the fact which first makes the history of these municipalities interesting.

There are two facts, however, which, even at this early date, begin to influence the internal history of the communes. These are the influence which the Church,[7] through its bishops, began to attain in the civil affairs of the country; and the idea beginning to gain currency that the locality where a number of individuals, however wretched in state, were collected together, would afford a safer refuge than the open country to the oppressed, the homeless and the outcast. I will briefly consider the latter first, as of less importance, though not unconnected with the former.

---

[7] The Christianity of the Lombards of the invasion was of the Arian form. Autari, who reigned from 584 to 591, married Theodolinda of Bavaria, and she first introduced orthodox Christianity. At the death of Autari she married Agiluf (591-615) duke of Turin, who was an Arian, but who pursued a mediative policy. During his reign a double ecclesiastical system, with orthodox and Arian bishops side by side, was maintained.

In the period of great confusion in all relations of property which ensued from the Lombard military system of small independent landholders and a few great overlords, with a nominal royal ownership of title, and before the feudal system was established, with its iron rules in regular working order, constant inequalities of wealth and consequent changes in the relative positions of individuals were sure to ensue. In practice if not in theory, might makes right in such a state of society. The weaker goes to the wall, and the stronger gains in strength by his downfall. Besides, it was long before the roving and predatory instinct of the barbarian was moderated; and his weaker neighbor was the natural prey of the more powerful landholder, an example not unfrequently set by the king himself. Now, if the weaker party remained to brave the attack and was conquered, he was reduced to a state of villeinage or of dependence more or less complete. If on the other hand he wished to escape this change of condition, where was he to find refuge? The only safe asylum in those days of rapine and violence was that offered by the Church and its precincts. The church of the greatest importance in the district, in this early age when no walled monasteries existed, would without doubt be that situated within the limits of the nearest town. To this haven then comes the outcast, hastily collecting his family and all of his wealth of a portable character; the country loses a small landed proprietor, but the town gains a citizen, a freeman, a member of the upper class.

Of course many of the fugitives who sought asylum in the towns were as low as the great numbers of the semi-servile population, but much that was new and of a better character and intelligence, and even a large amount of property, which later gave birth to commercial and other interests, were introduced by members of the higher classes fleeing from their more powerful neighbors. Also the human instinct of seeking fellowship in misfortune probably assisted in increasing the numbers which in times of trouble flocked towards the towns as a haven of refuge and a place to seek support. To see how they were in a measure enabled to attain these results, we must now consider the first of the two facts mentioned above, that is, the power in civil affairs gained by the bishops.

When the Lombards of the conquest, in their hatred of everything which savored of the old Roman civilization, overthrew all the established offices of city government to replace them with others of barbarian name and origin, or to leave them unfilled altogether, among the time-honored officers of the Roman rule was one whose powers were everywhere recognized, even if at present it is a little difficult to define with precision his duties. I refer to the *defensor urbis*. This office came into prominence when Roman despotism found that it was overreaching itself by grinding down the defenseless *curiae* below the margin of productiveness. The duties of the *defensor* were, as his name implies, to protect the powerless inhabitants of the cities against the exactions of the imperial ministers. He enjoyed many important privileges of jurisdiction, and these were materially increased by the legislation of Justinian; and soon the *defensor* became an important officer of the municipality.[8] What particularly concerns us is that he was the only municipal of-

[8] Justinian gave him the right to exercise, in reference to each city, the functions of the governor of the province, during the latter's absence; and granted him jurisdiction in all cases not involving a larger sum than 300 *aurei*. He had a certain amount of authority in

ficer who was elected not by the votes of the *curia* alone, but by those of the whole people forming the *municipium*, including the bishop and his clergy. Now in the period just preceding the invasion of the barbarians, the clergy alone possessed any energy and influence; so into their hands fell the control of this new institution, and consequently all that remained of life in the municipal system.

As in city matters these conditions remained unaltered after the coming of the Lombards, what was more natural than that the bishops should retain their moral position of defenders of the people, even if we admit that the form of the office fell with the old administration? To these considerations we may add two important facts: that the office of bishop was for a long time the only one in the election to which the people—and by this term I mean the people as a whole, not the *populus* of the old laws and charters—had any voice whatever; and that the bishop, from his spiritual position as pastor of the flock, and from his civil position as having great legal influence in the town and being probably the only man of superior intellect interested in the internal affairs of the community, was the proper and most effectual mediator between the people and their temporal rulers. Hence arose that important influence of the bishops which was to have so perceptible an effect on the subsequent development of the principles of liberty in the communes.

To appreciate properly, and to give the true value to this power in its later progress, we must remember one thing: that it did not have its origin by any seeking of power by either the Roman or the Ambrosian church as a body, in any concerted effort to extend the ecclesiastical power at the expense of the civil. It came from the spontaneous effort of the pastor, the natural and at that time the only protector of the people, trying to save his flock from the extortion and the injustice of their temporal rulers. In addition to this it must be remembered that at that time the office of the bishop was the only one where even the shadow of the democratic idea was preserved, the only one where the lowest of the people, theoretically at least, had a voice in the election. In later times, when the feudal system becomes established in its completeness, the position of the bishop undergoes a great change, as his relations to the state and to society become more complex in their character; and his importance in the community, while it at first increases, in time surely diminishes, under the influence of his double relation of lord and vassal to some higher temporal power. When he in his turn becomes the possessor of political power as a great baron or as head of a *civitas*, his interests, and consequently his influence, are concerned with intriguing and with efforts for his own political advancement, in many cases leaving but few traces of the old relation of "defender of the people." It is, however, of importance to note that this decline in his prominence in civil life is commensurate with the diminished need by the people of his protection, owing to the steady increase in the security and independence of their position.

---

criminal matters, and two apparitors were attached to his person. The *defensores* had two guarantees for their power and their independence. 1. They had the right of passing over the various degrees in the public administration, and of carrying their complaints at once before the praetorian prefect; this freed them from the jurisdiction of the provincial authorities. 2. They were elected by the general body of the inhabitants of the *municipium*.

To sum up briefly the chief characteristics of the early and obscure period which we have been considering, I think we can truly call it a transition period, and its history a tottering bridge from the dead Roman municipal system of the past, to the new state and city life of the future; from a state of society where, as we have seen, the city had changed from a political to an administrative division, to one where the city was to prepare itself again to claim, and eventually, by the growth of internal resources, to gain the lost function of sovereignty. The condition of the people during this time we have seen to be wretched in the extreme; the dismantled city but a bunch of comfortless dwellings; its inhabitants but a semi-servile population, with a small admixture of refugees of a better class; the city occupying but a subordinate place as part of the rural holding within whose limits it stood; whatever of wealth it contained an easy if not a legitimate prey to the turbulent spirits, whose mutual contests kept the surrounding country in a continual state of disturbance. The only men of any influence in the community we have seen to be the bishops, who, while steadily gaining in rank and power, stood forth as defenders of the people. During all this time, however, the new sap brought by the northern conquerors has been slowly but steadily entering into and forming the constitution of the people. The chaste and uncorrupted Northmen have by means of legitimate intermarriage with the best of the enervated inhabitants of the land, raised up an almost new race, who combine in their nature the humanizing effects of the old civilization with the love of independence and the temperate virtues of the northern conquerors, a race willing to benefit by the experience of the past, and resolved to carve out for itself a new and independent future.

PART II.

ELEMENTARY SOURCES OF MUNICIPAL UNITY IN LOMBARD AND FRANKISH TIMES.

In the second part of this paper we have to consider a period of development rather than one of transition, of growth rather than of change. We have before us the task of tracing the advance from a period of barbarism to one when the feudal system had obtained an almost complete domination over the social system of Europe. Considering the principles which lay at the base of the society of new Europe, this system is a natural, indeed an unavoidable evolution from the stage of barbarism and social disorganization. The confusion in all social and economic relations consequent on the combination of the old and the new elements in European life, had led to a state of disintegration that could not continue. A new regulative force was required which would at the same time have power sufficient to control the various warring elements with which it had to deal and reduce them to some sort of harmony, and yet which would not in its nature be in opposition to the decentralizing spirit and the idea of individual independence, which formed the most marked characteristic of the dominant element of the new society. Feudalism sprang from the midst of barbarism not by a sudden birth, but by a growth at once natural and necessary: natural, because it was but a regulation by law of conditions produced by the character of the people and their mode of life; necessary, because the progress of civilization was carrying society ahead of the stage of anarchy and barbarism in which the overthrow of the old regime had left it.

The economic changes which were produced by the transition to the new principles represented by the feudal system, are as great and in their way as important as the political ones. When we say that feudalism represents the transfer of the dominant power from a central head to scattered members, from the capital to the castles, we speak of it in its most prominent, its political character. But we must not forget that this transfer also meant a great economic change in the organization of society: that it meant a transfer of the seat of economic importance from the city to the country; the spirit of the times requiring, especially in the earlier stages of the development of the institution, that the seat of wealth should follow the seat of power. I note this now because we shall soon have occasion to consider how important a factor, in the earliest period of the development of the cities, their entire lack of prominence in both political and economic affairs was to prove itself. Under the old Roman system, as we have seen, the city was the important unit: Rome was a subduer and an upbuilder of cities. Under the new Teutonic element the land is what is brought into prominence, and the possessor of it into power.

The dominant member of society is the landowner and not the citizen. In ancient society the "citizen" need own no land; in the modern society of the feudal age, the "gentleman" could not be such without owning land.

This opposition between the citizen, the burgher, and the landowner, the baron, leads us to a conclusion of the utmost importance to the whole study of city life during the middle ages. We note the universal prevalence of the *forms* characteristic of the feudal system, and from this we conclude that its *principles* were as universally adopted. Now this is to a certain extent an error. There were certain institutions which from the very nature of their origin and of the principles on which they were based, must have been, at once in their idea and in their structure, opposed to the fundamental principle of feudalism. The Roman Church, for example, conformed itself to the forms and customs of this system, but never lost its structural unity and centralization, ideas founded on principles which stood in direct opposition to those of feudalism. So it was, though perhaps in a less degree, with the cities. Though adapting themselves in many ways to feudal forms, here the idea of democracy was as strong in its opposition to the dominant principle of feudalism, as ever was that of centralization in the Church. The people, in their own conception at least, stood out as an organic unity, and they considered their rights and duties as matters which concerned them collectively, not separately, as the commonwealth, not as individuals. Of course it was long before any such opposition assumed a definite form and shape, before even the people became conscious of its existence; but what I wish to point out is, that it was there in fact from the beginning, and must have formed a structural part of the development of city life in the middle ages.

In outlining the course of the history of institutions, it is seldom that we are so fortunate as to find definite landmarks by which we can accurately mark the chronological course of their development. The giving of definite dates for the progress of ideas is in most cases both misleading and illusory, as, except in instances of violent revolution, changes are apt to be gradual, rather than immediate and arbitrary. But we can indicate the periods of progress by comparing them with the contemporary political changes, and roughly designate their eras by the dates of prominent political events. In doing this, however, we must always remember that the dates given, while definite from a political standpoint, are in most cases, from an institutional standpoint, only indicative of a more or less extended period of change. This fact being recognized, let us proceed to examine the changes introduced into Italy by the Carlovingian rulers, and the condition of the society upon which these changes were engrafted.

When in the year 773-774, Charlemagne, in pursuance of his idea of universal empire, and aiding the Pope as "Patricius" of Rome, entered Lombardy with his army, took Pavia after a siege of six months, and shut up Desiderius in a monastery, he found in Lombard society a well defined, if not a perfectly developed system. In all their relations with other nations, the evidence of history proves the Franks to have been a conquering rather than a colonizing race; consequently we may expect to find that in their conquest of Lombardy, they rather gave her only new rulers without materially interfering with the condition of the inhabitants or altering their mode of life. The institutions of the Frankish nation were similar, in many important matters identical, with those of their neighbors across the Alps; so the changes introduced into the Lombard system by the Carlovingian rule are, with a few exceptions, not such as affect the integral structure of society, but for the most part only such as refer to the character and position of the central or ruling power.

I say with a few exceptions, for among these very exceptions are to be found certain alterations in the government of the cities, introduced chiefly by the necessities of the system of central government established by Charlemagne, but also partly by the claims of individuality, which at this time first began in the cities timidly to call for recognition. The very relation of the cities with the central power seems to me to be a much more important factor in their growth during this period than is generally supposed; for it not only secured to their inhabitants better chances of justice and protection from the powerful local rulers, but, bringing them, through certain officers, into direct connection with the head of the state, added not a little to their moral importance, a condition which in a growing community is always closely followed by an increase of material importance. According to their size they were the seats of courts of varying degrees of importance, and from them as centres proceeded the acts of royal officers, both ordinary and extraordinary. Ticinum was the capital, where in Lombard times the king had his palace.[9]

For a satisfactory study of the development of the municipal institutions we need a thorough understanding of the organization of society at this time, and especially of the relations which the municipal and rural communities bore to one another and to the government. I will endeavor to give, therefore, a description of Lombard society about the close of the eighth century, as brief as is consistent with a clear understanding of these relations, and as complete as the great difficulties of the subject will permit, pointing out, whenever they are authentically traceable, the changes introduced in consequence of the Carlovingian conquest.

When we reach in Lombard history the period when the power of the native kings was first overthrown by foreign arms, we are no longer confronted by many of the problems which necessarily formed an important part of the earlier portions of our investigation. I mean the problems which arise in a state of society where the mass of individuals forming it is made up of two elements, a conquering, dominant one, and a conquered, subject one. During the two centuries elapsed since the Lombard barbarians conquered Italy, the two races, originally so different in their ideas and in their character, so opposed in their customs and in their nature, have been slowly but surely blending together, on the strength of common environment and by the necessities of mutual relations: so that by the last half of the eighth century, we can truly say that national differences, as such, have disappeared, and left behind them a single race, a combination but still a unity. We no longer have to deal with a double nationality, with the northern conquerors and their southern victims, with the oppressed and their oppressors. In considering the development of the institutional life of the people, we need no longer seek for differences, but may assume the easier task of tracing similarities. In a word, we

---

[9] *Paulus Diaconus*: Lib. V., 7, 17, 18.

no longer speak of Lombards and of Romans, but describe all that remains of both by the new word *Italians.*

It is not within the scope of this enquiry to trace the various steps or indicate the various influences, the civilizing effect of the Church, the restraining power of the law, by which this complete amalgamation of two distinct races became an accomplished fact; we need only to note that the unity of the race was achieved. Even Macchiavelli recognizes this fact and, speaking of the time of the Carlovingian conquest, in the brief review of the history of all Italy which forms the first part of the first book of the "Florentine History," he truly says that, after two hundred and twenty-two years of occupation by the Lombards, "they retained nothing of the foreigner save the name."[10]

But we must always bear in mind that it was not a process of absorption of one race by another, but a process of combination, of amalgamation; a levelling process, by which some members of the conquered people, by natural and economic causes, were raised to the level of their superiors; and on the other hand, some of the conquerors, by reason of similar causes, fell to the rank of the subject population. By manumission and by the various forms of vassalage more or less honorable, and by gaining some economic importance by trade and other means, many of the descendants of the Roman population gained admission to the ranks of the Arimanni, and obtained the full franchise by the possession of landed property. By forfeitures, consequent poverty and ultimate pauperization, many of the Lombard stock lost their rank and their lands and entered the same state of vassalage with the great body of the people. We see evidences of this change, this levelling up and levelling down, all through the military code of Liutprand, and in the later one of Aistulf can even more distinctly trace its progress; and without entering into further detail, we can definitely state that, by the time we are now considering, all traces of distinct race-origin had disappeared in the mass of the people, and the only safe distinction that we can draw is to say that among the families of the dukes and greater nobles, the Lombard stock was preserved comparatively pure, and that the serf population was, generally speaking, of Roman descent.[11]

---

[10] His words are: "Erano stati i Longobardi dugento ventidue anni in Italia, e di già non ritenevano di forastieri altro che il nome." —*Nicolò Macchiavelli*: Istorie Fiorentine, Lib. I. *vid.* Opere, Vol. III., p. 219 (ed. Milano, 1804).

[11] It is difficult to draw any picture of the different ranks of society at this period, which would at once be perfectly accurate, and yet definite enough to give entire satisfaction to the student.

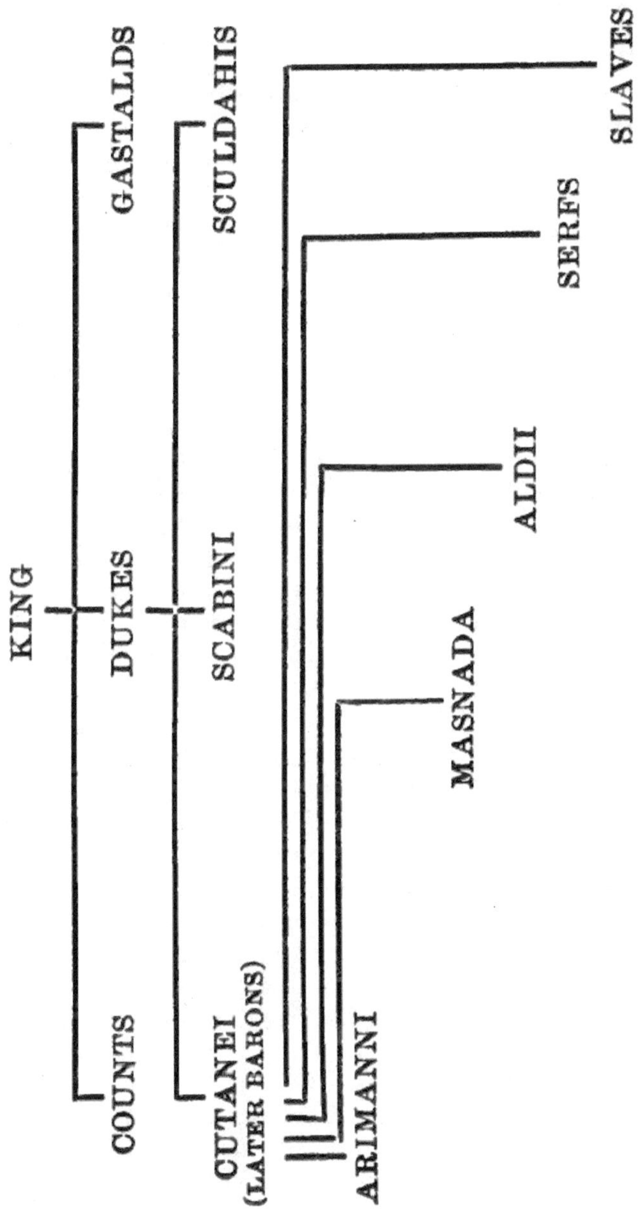

The above table, while its divisions must not be taken too literally, will, I think, give some indication of the estimation in which the various classes of society were held. It is too early yet in the development of the feudal system to say that the derivation lines show the course of an absolute feudal tenure, and they are not meant for that purpose, but simply to indicate the succession of the inequalities of rank.

Turning now to the territorial divisions of the country at this period, we find them practically unchanged. The *civitas* still stands as the sectional unit; the territory with its city still represents the administrative division of the state. It is fundamental to a correct understanding of the early development of communal institutions that we should have a thorough knowledge of the meaning of this term *civitas*; of the extent of its application and of its limitations. I used the words "territory with its city" in defining the administrative division of the state, and perhaps this term describes the *civitas* better than any single word would do. In the Roman municipal system we have the city with its surrounding territory, over which extends the jurisdiction of the *curia*; in the Lombard system we have the territory, the land, in some part of which is located a city, a fortified place.

This is to my mind the important point which settles satisfactorily the vexed question of the dominance or the disappearance of Roman influences. The institutions of the Lombards were similar in character to those of the other Germanic races, and the continuance of any overruling municipal influence among them would have done violence alike to their traditions and to the nature of their race. The old municipal predominance as a system disappeared, the old municipal divisions and many of the minor forms and offices as a fact remained. It is these latter which give some color to the arguments of writers like Savigny,[12] who endeavor to maintain the continuance of the old Roman *curia*. They find evidence of the continuance of old boundaries, of many old names and many old executive functions, and fail to appreciate that the principle which lay back of and was making use of these old forms as convenient channels for the expression of its power and of its control, was an entirely new one, based on ideas fundamentally opposed to those of the civilization it had conquered. This slight warning is necessary so as to avoid any error in the conception of the significance to be attached to the geographical limits of the divisions of territory we are considering.

The word *civitas* has the same signification as *comitatus*, when that word was used with the meaning of a territorial division; and included all the territory, with its lands, its villages, its fortified places and its city, which came under the jurisdiction of a *dux* or *judex*, or in Frankish times of a count, when we are strictly justified in giving it the more familiar name of *county*. From this we trace the Italian word *contado*, by the steps *comitatu, comitato, contato, contado*. The land division here indicated is indifferently called in the Lombard records *territorium, fines, civitas*, or *judiciaria*. The identity of all these terms admits of easy proof from all the documents, public and private; and numberless instances could be cited showing an interchange of terms in describing the same locality.

I will mention in illustration of this fact the rather neat example of a document of the year 762, published by Brunetti[13] in his Codice Diplomatico Toscano, in which three of these terms are used interchangeably in the space of a few lines. It is a contract by which a certain Arnifrid, an inhabitant of Clusium—the modern Chiusi—who "in clusino territorio ... natus fuit," pledges himself to live on a certain property, and says "nullam conbersationem facias nec in clusio nec in alia civitate

---

[12] Geschichte des römischen Rechts im Mittelalter, *passim.*
[13] *Brunetti*: Cod. Diplom. Toscan. Firenze, 1806, Docum. No. 44.

habitandum, nisi.... &c.," and promises to pay fifty *solidi* if "pro eo quod ipsa pecunia demittere presumbsero aut de judiciaria vestra suaninse exire voluero." The contract is "Actum in civitate suana." We here see the words *territorium* and *civitas* both applied to the territory of Chiusi, and the words *judiciaria* and *civitas* both applied to the territory of Siena, and we only need to remember that things which are equal to the same thing are equal to each other, to recognize the identity of the terms. If we look at document number eight in the same collection,[14] we will further see the territory of Chiusi referred to as "fines clusinas."

Hand-in-hand with the growth of episcopal organization we see another term coming into use in connection with the same land division, and this also is an administrative one, but of the church simply, and only made use of by conversion or carelessly when applied to a civil area. I mean the *districtus*, which term is properly applicable only to the jurisdiction of a bishop, and designates the limits of his episcopal power, that is, his diocese. The reasons for this term being used in later times occasionally for the civil division, the *civitas*, are twofold. They result, firstly, from the confusion which arose between matters of civil and ecclesiastical jurisdiction, when political power was given to a large number of the bishops, and when they united to their religious duties as pastor, the judicial and sometimes even some of the military duties of *comes* and *judex*. And secondly, in the important fact that in almost all cases the boundaries of a bishop's diocese coincided more or less exactly with the limits of the authority of the state officers; so that the division which should be called a *civitas* or *territorium* from the point of view of civil government, should be called a *districtus* from that of ecclesiastical government.

Where we find at once the most important and, if not rightly understood, the most perplexing traces of the survival of the old Roman municipal system, is in this matter of territorial boundaries. According to the Roman system, as we have seen, the city was the important administrative unit, and each city was surrounded by a belt of rural lands, more or less large according to the size and importance of the city itself. This of course resulted in a division of the whole country into a number of districts whose boundaries were definitely marked, perhaps even jealously guarded. Now, when the Lombards took possession of the country, while they rejected the principle of the municipal unit, as foreign to the character and instincts of their race, they could not fail to see the practical utility of using, and the actual difficulty of overthrowing, a system of land division which custom and authority had united in rendering alike definite and convenient. What was the result? They made use of the old boundary lines, leaving their limits, as far as we can judge, untouched, and substituted as the fundamental principle of their administration, in place of the Roman idea of the *municipium*, the thoroughly Teutonic idea of the *civitas* or country district. Coincident with these time-honored boundaries which served to mark the limits of the jurisdiction of the duke and the *judex*, are to be found those of the ecclesiastical power, of the bishop's diocese.

This statement is confirmed by the many charters, immunities, etc., addressed to the episcopal authorities; and direct proof of it may be had by reference to the controversy which arose in the first half of the eighth century between the bishops

---

[14] *Idem.* Docum. No. 8.

of Arezzo and Siena, which dispute was based on the fact that for reasons definitely stated these two dioceses formed an exception to the general rule. The strength of the proof lies in this exception, which had a well-known cause for its origin. Some of the documents[15] in the case, of the year 715, show that the bishop of Siena claimed for his jurisdiction certain churches which belonged to the diocese of Arezzo, basing his claim solely on the ground that these churches were situated in the *territorium* of Siena. The bishop of Arezzo, on the other hand, claims them as part of his diocese, on the ground that they had formed part of it ever since the beginning of Lombard rule in Italy; and—which is the part of importance to us—gives as the only reason for their having been attached to the diocese of a neighboring *territorium*, the fact that at that early date there was no bishop in the *territorium* of Siena. That a claim of such a character should have been based on the argument of the natural coincidence of the boundaries of *territorium* and diocese, is sufficient proof of the identity of these limits at that age. In a bull of the year 752,[16] Pope Stephen II. decides to adhere to the already existing diocesan divisions, and adjudges to the bishop of Arezzo the churches "quae esse manifestum est sub consecratione et regimine praefatae S. Aretinae Ecclesiae, territorium vero est prefatae nominatae Civitatis Senensis."

We see then the perpetuation of the old Roman land divisions in the new commonwealth through the medium of the *civitas* and the diocese. How long these divisions remained intact and what were the causes and the extent of their final overthrow, forms part of the history of the later development of the Italian communes. Here I will simply indicate the fact, that among the reasons which led in most instances to a departure from this system of land boundaries, are to be found some of the most important causes for the development of freedom and independent jurisdiction among the cities. It is to the destruction of this identity of interests and of government which existed between country and city, that is owed the ultimate predominance of the latter, and its regaining its ancient position of a self-centered unity; although in its new form we find this depending on the principle of individual liberty, instead of being based on the principle of government by a central power. Whether this emancipation from the bonds of a rural dependence was brought about by the practice later entered upon, of breaking up the counties into a number of smaller units with the so-called "rural counts," each ruling over a *castellum* or fortified village; or by the fact that many of the bishops obtained political as well as religious control over a city and a limited area of the surrounding country, generally extending only three or five miles beyond the city walls; or whether this freedom was the result of the spontaneous growth of civic and economic life within the city itself; or finally, whether it came from a combination of all these and many minor causes, is a question which—for the early period of the development at least—the progress of our investigation will answer for itself.

It will, however, be impossible for us to understand thoroughly the relations of the city under Lombard and Frankish rule to the central and to the local government, unless we know somewhat of the local and state officers who exercised jurisdiction within the territorial limits just described. By a consideration of their

[15] *Brunetti*: Cod. Diplom. Toscan. Docum. Nos. 6-10.
[16] *Idem.* Docum. No. 43.

special powers and of their special duties, we must learn all that we can know with any degree of certainty with regard to the position of the city in these times. With this in mind, let us first examine the office whose functions it is at once the most difficult and the most important for us to understand in all its bearings—that of the *Judex*. We must consider it not only in the relation which it bears to the higher grade of officers, the Lombard duke and the Frankish count, but also in its relation with the lower officials who severally enjoyed more or less of the powers attached to its possession, namely, the gastald, the sculdahis, the scabino, and even the rural counts and the bishop. And in tracing its development we must note the influence it bore on the growth of the municipal idea, and also its connection with the political jurisdiction, commonly combined with it in the person of a single official.

In considering the institutions of a comparatively crude state of society, such as existed in Europe in the early middle ages, it is misleading if not impossible to differentiate to any great extent the various functions and kinds of power which were commonly centered in the same individual. Consequently the only safe way to give a clear idea of the position and the powers of the *judex*, is to give a description of the various offices to which judicial authority was attached, in degrees more or less complete, corresponding to the social and political importance of the person exercising this authority.

In the Lombard system, at the head of each *civitas*, as lord and as judge, was the *dux*, or duke. His title and his office being but the relic of his original high position of leadership in the army of the invasion, when his command was only subject to that of the king, the leader-in-chief of the army-nation and head of the military constitution, he held directly from the king, attended the royal *placita* as the king's vassal, and held *placita* of his own within his own jurisdiction, and over which he presided in person. Beyond the duties of his own particular jurisdiction his chief office was to assist the king by his presence and his counsel, when the king gave his judgments at the annual assembly in March, at the capital Ticinum. The importance of this concurrence of the *judices* in all the king's decrees and official acts is illustrated by the fact that cases are rare in which this concurrence remains unmentioned. The usual practice is to introduce in the prologue which is commonly attached to the laws given out during each year of the king's reign, after the mention of the date "Kalendiis Martiarum," some such expression as "cum nostris Judicibus";[17] or "ad nos conjungerentur Judices";[18] or "per suggestionem Judicum";[19] to which is sometimes added the formula "omniumque consensum,"[20] or "cum reliquis nostris Langobardis fidelis." That legislation was not considered valid until such consent and advice was obtained, we can see from the prologue to the laws issued in the thirteenth year of the reign of Liutprand, in which he refers to certain important "causae" which had come under his jurisdiction, and for which additional legislation was necessary, the laws already existing failing to

---

[17] *Liutprandi*: Leg. Long. Prolog. Anni XVI. et XV. et al. Vid. *Muratori*: Script. Rer. Ital., Tom. I., P. II., p. 15, et seq.

[18] *Liutprandi*: Leg. Prolog. Anni XIII. Vid. *Muratori*: Script. Rer. Ital., Tom. I., P. II., p. 15.

[19] *Crimoaldi*: Leg. Prolog. Vid. *Muratori* op. cit. Tom. I., P. II., p. 49.

[20] *Crimoaldi*: Leg. Prolog. Vid. *Muratori* op. cit. Tom. I., P. II., p. 49.

reach them. To meet the exigency new laws are enacted, but the king especially states that the cases must remain in abeyance until the new laws are confirmed by the *judices* at the next assembly in March. In speaking of these "causae" in the above-mentioned prologue to the laws, he says: "Proinde providimus eas usque ad suprascriptum diem Kalendii Martiarum suspendere dum usque nostri ad nos conjungerentur judices," etc.[21] This attendance at the royal *placita* represents the most important of the legislative duties of the *judex* outside of his own jurisdiction.

Of other duties which caused him to leave the seat of his authority, the only ones we need here consider are his military duties; and with regard to these it will be sufficient to point out that the *judex* was the leader in war of the vassals and lesser lords, and indeed of all the inhabitants of the *judiciaria* who were entitled or compelled, by the forms of their tenure, to bear arms. Ample proof of this is to be found throughout the law codes, but we need not pause to cite such confirmation, if we remember the natural evolution of the office of *dux* from his position in the original Lombard military system. As a good example of this military leadership we may refer to the provisions of the twenty-ninth law in the sixth book of the laws of Liutprand.[22]

What is of the greatest importance to us, however, in bringing out the relations of the cities to the rest of the community in Lombard and Frankish times, is the position of the *judex* as duke and as count within his own *judiciaria*, that is, within the *civitas* of which he was both lord and judge. It was through him, or perhaps I should say chiefly through him, that the city was at this period connected with the state; and it was principally by the exercise of the functions of his office that the city formed a part of the state. His official residence, in the majority of cases, and his courts, were situated within the city's limits; thus making the official machinery of government a part of the city life, and causing the city to become an actual if not a legally recognized part of the constitution of the state. As far as this investigation is concerned, this represents the prominent feature of the power and position of the head of the *civitas*. We must be careful, however, to avoid any confusion of ideas as to the importance which it gave to the city as a municipal unit or as a corporation. It was in no way what we could call a municipal government, even admitting a rather loose interpretation of the term, as the supporters of the theory of the survival of the Roman curial system would have us believe.[23] The *judex* may be called "the highest municipal officer among the Lombards," and this designation still be correct, though perhaps misleading. He was the highest officer of the locality, and his official duties were for the most part carried on within the city; but the leading fact we must keep prominently before us is, that he was the head of the whole *civitas*, and not in any sense of the city as such: and further, that his powers over the rural portions of the *civitas* were in no sense added to any purely municipal powers he may have possessed; but, on the contrary, if we are to draw any distinctions, the municipality formed a part of the land division. That the whole *civitas* was commonly named after the largest town contained within

[21] *Liutprandi*: Leg. Prolog. ad Lib. III. Vid. *Muratori*: Script. Rer. Ital., Tom. I., Pars II., p. 15.

[22] *Muratori*: Script. Rer. Ital., T. II., Pars II.

[23] *Savigny*: Gesch. des röm. Rechts im Mittelalter, S. 422 et al.

its borders, and that the seat of power was generally placed within the city walls, are facts too evidently brought about by motives of convenience and expediency and by the force of old association, to lead to any confusion in appreciating the proper place of the city. Where there were to be found buildings suitable for the residence of the *dux*, and where was located the largest collection of individuals, was manifestly the most appropriate place for holding the courts and settling the disputes of the inhabitants of the whole *civitas*, and this formed a natural centre for the machinery of government. But every inhabitant of the *civitas* had equal rights with the townsman proper, and, as in the old Greek πόλις, the most remote countryman dwelling on the borders of the *civitas*, if he possessed the franchise, was as much a citizen of Padua, Siena or Milan, as if he dwelt within the walls of the city which gave its name to the whole *civitas*.

A consideration of these facts brings out two important points, which I will briefly indicate before passing on to a little more detailed treatment of the powers and the duties of the *judex*. In the first place it has been made clear that at the time under discussion nothing that could correctly be called a "municipal system" existed in Lombardy, and the city, *as such*, had no independent existence or independent relations with the state. And secondly, it cannot but be manifest that the position that the city did occupy as actual, if not necessarily as legal, centre from which issued all the administrative functions of the district, the residence of the chief authority and the seat of his courts, would have a marked tendency to increase slowly, perhaps imperceptibly at first, the importance of its position at once in the *civitas* and in the state, and at the same time to improve the character of its inhabitants and in time increase their wealth. That this ultimately came about the development of the later independent communal life is a proof, and the tardy steps by which this was attained but serve to show the difficulties consequent on so slight and so feeble a beginning.

The obscurity which promptly descends on the brain of the intelligent reader who endeavors to gain a clear idea of the state of society or of the administration of government in these early ages of Italian history, makes the careful student very skeptical of any precise presentation he may find of them, and causes him to be particularly cautious and proportionately diffident in making, himself, any very definite statements concerning them. If he be a wise man and wish to make his investigation of some use to others, he frequently says "it seems probable," and he particularly avoids mentioning dates which are fixed and immovable. If this may be said of all matters not belonging simply to the narrative portions of history at this period, particularly true is it of the different functions attributed to various officers of local government, whose very titles we sometimes have to infer from their duties, and whose duties we often have to infer from their titles.

To these the *judex*, though the most prominent, cannot be said to form an exception. That he was the head of the district judicial system has in part been already shown, and will come out more clearly when we come to define the powers of some of his subordinates. His leadership in war we have seen to be but the natural continuance of his original office; and that as *dux* he was to be ranked among the first nobles of the land, the "optimates," the "viri illustres," we can see from the following passage in the laws of Liutprand, when in the prologue to the third book already quoted, he gives forth the edict with the judges as "una cum illustribus viris optimatibus meis ex Neustriae et Austriae et Tusciae partibus vel universis nobilibus Langobardis."[24] Although the position of the *duces* as nobles of the land never altered, their power relative to that of the king suffered many modifications. The ducal power—"principes" of Tacitus—preceding among the Lombards that of the king, we see the dukes exercising much greater control in the earlier stages of the monarchy: even, on the death of Clefis—576—actually establishing a sort of aristocratic republic, under the leadership of thirty dukes, which lasted for ten years; after which time, on the event of a dangerous war with the Greeks and the Franks, Authari, the son of Clefis, gained the throne by election; the dukes giving up to him, says Paulus Diaconus,[25] the half of their estates for the support of his dignity, retaining, however, the rest, not as servants of the king, but as "principes" of the people, an important distinction. Agiluf—591 to 615—originally duke of Turin, met with much opposition from the power of the dukes; but when we come to the time of Rhotari—636 to 652—we find their power already declining, and in the eighth century, as for example under Liutprand—712 to 736—the laws show them reduced to the position of the other *judices*, but still representing a high aristocracy whose consent was, as we have seen, necessary to all acts of the king.

The most important of the functions of the *dux* as *judex* was holding the *Curtis Regia* or *Curtis Ducalis*, in the largest city or "urbs" of every *civitas*. Here, in conjunction with his subordinates, he heard all cases which did not go up to the king for judgment, and here was centered the fiscal administration of the *civitas*. To describe in detail the composition of these *curtes*, their jurisdiction and methods of procedure, would require a whole chapter of no mean proportions, and however interesting in itself, would be out of place in the present investigation. All that it is needful for us to consider is the relation of these *curtes* to the municipalities in which they were located. Of their location within the city walls the proofs to be found in numbers of the old documents are to me conclusive. I will give a few examples, however, commencing with two from the documents which have already been quoted from Brunetti, relating to the dispute between the bishops of Siena and Arezzo. In the first of these[26] we see that in the year 715, the king's *major-domus* Ambrosius interferes "in Curte a Domini Regis" at Siena, in opposition to the local bishop and gastald; and in the second[27] we find the royal notary Gunthram forbidding a fresh examination of witnesses "in Curte Regia Senensis." In a document of the next year[28]—716—we find "Ebugansus, Notarius regiae Curtis," taking part in the procedure in a case between the bishops of Pistoia and Lucca; and a little later, in the year 756, is mention of an exchange of property between "civitis regia lucencis" and the church situated in that city.[29] In the "Opusculum

---

[24] *Muratori*: Script. Rer. Ital., Tom. I., Pars II., p. 15.

[25] *Paulus Diaconus*: De Gest. Langobard., Lib. III., cap. 16.

[26] *Brunetti*: Cod. Diplom. Toscan. Docum. No. 6, anni 715.

[27] *Ibid.*: Cod. Diplom. Toscan. Docum. No. 8, anni 715.

[28] *Ibid.*: Docum. No. 11, anni 716.

[29] *Ibid.*: Docum. No. 50, anni 756.

de Fundat. Monast. Nonantulae," published by Muratori,[30] we find a donation by King Aistulf to that monastery: "prope castellum Aginulfi, quod pertinet de curte nostra lucense, et duas casas masaritias de ipsa curte"; and "granum ilium, quod annue colligitur de portatico, in Curte nostra, quae sita est in Civitate Nova."[31] In Carlovingian times Charles the Bald, in the year 875, in the "Chronica Farfense,"[32] appears as saying, "in Curte nostra infra Castrum Viterbense": elsewhere "curtis regie Viturbensis" is spoken of[33]: and later, in 899, Berenger gives to the bishop of Florence "terram ... pertinentem de curte Regis istae Florentiae"[34]: and finally, not to multiply examples, I will mention a privilege of Karloman's, published by Ughelli[35], by which he gives to the bishop of Parma certain regalia: "id est curtem regiam extructam infra civitatem Parmam cum omne officio suo," etc. From even these few instances we can see the connection between the *Curtis Regia* and the city which gave its name to the *civitas*, a connection the importance of which we must not fail to appreciate, in consideration of the great influence which it exercised in the future development of the municipal unit from a beginning so insignificant.

Of some importance in connection with the early history of the cities are the questions which arise in relation to the fiscal duties and privileges of the *curtes regia* and its officers. In it was centered the fiscal administration of the kingdom; and its officers, in the various grades from the *dux* downward, received and were responsible for the revenues of the state. So prominent a part belonged to this form of the functions of the *curtes* that it is quite common to hear the revenues themselves, by a transposition of terms, called by that name, or by that of *palatium*, a word sometimes found even for the *curtes regia* in their proper general sense; but this, from what I have been able to gather concerning its legitimate use, should properly be applied only to the residence, or by conversion the revenues of the king himself[36]. What is of interest to us in this matter is the fact that the *curtis regia* fell heir to the *publicum* or communal property of the old Roman *curia*, when these were overthrown by the Lombard conquest.

In considering this phase of civil administration under the Lombard system, we are again brought face to face with the old question of the survival or non-sur-

[30] *Muratori*: Script. Rer. Ital., Tom. I., Pars II., p. 192E.

[31] *Muratori*: Antiq. Ital. Diss. II., p. 186.

[32] *Muratori*: Script. Rer. Ital., Tom. II., Pars II., p. 409.

[33] In a donation to "Aimo Voltarius, abitator castrii Viterbii." Vid, *Troya*: Della Condizione, etc., p. 361. Docum. No. 6, anni 775.

[34] *Ughelli*: Italia Sacra, Tom. III., p. 28.

[35] *Ibid.*: Tom. II., p. 145.

[36] The word *palatium* in the signification of *fiscus* is perhaps more frequently used by the Frankish kings than by the Lombard. See a *privilegium* granted to the nuns of the Posterla di Pavia by Lothar I. in the year 839, in which it appears that any one infringing its privileges must pay seventy pounds of the best gold, to be applied "medietatem Palatio nostro, et medietatem parti ejusdem monasterii." Vid. *Muratori*: Antiq. Ital. Diss. XVI., Tom I., P. I., p. 233. Also several diplomas of Charles the Fat, and others make use of the same term. The word *camera* for *fiscus* as the imperial treasury, was probably not used before the time of Lewis II.; the first authentic use of it in that sense being probably a diploma of that monarch of the year 894, where he says that one hundred pounds of gold are to be paid "medietatem Imperiali Camere et medietatem suprataxatae Angilberge." Vid. *Muratori*: loc. cit. p. 234.

vival of corporate existence among the cities. For if it could be proved that the municipality in its corporate capacity retained the communal property and administered it, there would appear to be good grounds for the assertion of the continuance of some form of quasi-independent municipal government; but if, on the other hand, it were found that the property of the municipality passed to the new head of local administration or to the central power, it would be evident that the continuance of the municipal system as such was a logical impossibility; for, deprived at once of its property and of its revenues, it would have had no vitality to keep it from a speedy end.

In investigating a question of this nature from the sources at our disposal in a period of history so obscure, we cannot expect to find any definite statements sufficiently precise to set at rest at once all opposition and discussion; but after considering the character of the people we are investigating and studying their institutions, and after a careful examination of the laws and records which form the sources of our information, we are, I think, in a position to be able to give a sufficiently decided opinion as to whether a particular set of facts or conditions could possibly have existed in a state of development and in a society of a given character. Thus it is in regard to the matter in hand. From the numberless cases in which the *publicum* is mentioned in the documents from which we draw our materials, it seems to me possible for a critical examiner to come to but one conclusion, if, as is quite essential, he take into consideration the unmistakable spirit of these writings, and if he give a legitimate interpretation to the various terms employed. To cite in direct proof any individual instance is, perhaps, impossible; but indirect evidence is forthcoming in abundance, and of a character to be, to me at least, entirely conclusive. The conclusion reached is, then, that the king and the dukes were the successors of the old *curia* in the possession and the administration of all properties and revenues, taxes and fines formerly belonging to the organized corporations of the Roman municipalities, and that the *curtes regiae* were the channel through which these were collected, divided and expended.

The grounds on which this assertion is based are the continual recurrence of examples of functions of a fiscal character being exercised by the head of the *civitas* and his officers, and by them alone; and it appears to me that it could only be by a complete misunderstanding of the spirit of the early writings, and by a comprehensive misapplication of the terms used in them, that these functions could be referred to any other power. These functions of the administration may be grouped under three main heads, viz: 1. Fines and forfeitures, which, of course, played a very prominent part under the Teutonic system of composition for offenses of a criminal nature; 2. Taxes and privileges, by which is meant feudal rights, dues, etc.; and 3. Buildings and lands belonging to the crown or to the head of the *civitas* as a public officer.

Of the fines and forfeitures paid into the *publicum*, we find that a part went to the royal treasury and a part to the *judex*, and in some cases to the informer or the prosecuting officer; and at different times we find these proportionate amounts definitely defined—as, for instance, in the time of Charlemagne two parts went to the king and one part to the count who acted as *judex*;[37] this we know from two of the Lombard laws of that emperor.[38] In one of these,[39] speaking of those who evaded military service, he says: "Heribannum comes exactare non praesumat: nisi Missus noster prius Heribannum ad partem nostram recipiat, et ei," the Count, "suam tertiam partem exinde per jussionem nostram donet."[40] We even find evidence of quite a large amount of liberty used by the *duces* in the ultimate disposal of property coming under their jurisdiction by forfeiture, the more powerful making use of it precisely as if it were private property. For example, in the Chronica Farfensis[41] appears a case judged by Hildeprandus, *dux* of Spoleto, in the year 787. A certain nun named Alerona, for having married a man named Rabennonus, "secundum legem omnis substantia ipsius ad Publicum devoluta est"; a little later Rabennonus, for having killed a man, "medietas omnis illius substantiae ad Publicum devoluta est." In consequence, in poetic justice and for the good of his soul and the king's, Hildeprandus quite arbitrarily presents "omnem praedictam illorum substantiam, qualiter secundum legem juste et rationabiliter, ad Publicum devoluta est," to the Monastery of Farfa "pro mercede Domnorum nostrorum Regum et nostra." Here, as in many other cases, we see the *dux* making gifts of property belonging clearly to the *publicum*, to persons favored by him and for his own benefit. Such a condition of affairs would certainly never have existed had public property been administered by authority other than that of the *dux*.

With regard to the revenues falling under the second of the rough divisions we have indicated—taxes and privileges—it is easier to see why differences of opinion should have arisen; for here, especially in matters relating to the collecting of taxes and dues, we are confronted with the names of a large number of lesser officials and subordinates of the *judex*, some of which are undoubtedly taken from the like officers existing in the old Roman curial system. But this survival of names, and in some instances of offices, need cause us no alarm, for it coincides exactly with the theory presented, namely, a continuance of many of the old *forms* of administration controlled by an entirely new *principle* of government. There are certain minor functions necessary for the support of the state which must be carried on in much the same manner, whatever be the character of the governing power—certain subordinate offices whose duties must be performed under a republic or under a despotism. Taxes may be collected by widely differing methods under the two systems, but there must always be the tax collector and the tax assessor. We can, however, see at a glance the weakness of any argument which contends that because the name and even the general duties of the tax gatherer were the same in each case, that the whole system of administration of the taxes or of the community were necessarily identical or even closely allied in character.

It is here we see the weakness of those writers who insist upon the continu-

---

[37] From *Otto of Freising*, De Gest. Freder., Lib I., cap. 31, we know that the same distribution took place in Hungary, which was divided into seventy *comitates*; "et de omni justitia ad Fiscum Regium duas lucri partes cedere, tertiam tantum Comiti remanere."

[38] *Charlemagne*: Leg. Lomb. Nos. 127 and 128.

[39] Lex No. 128.

[40] *Muratori*: Diss. Ant. Ital. Dissert. VIII., Tom. I., P. I., p. 96.

[41] *Muratori*: Script. Rer. Ital., Tom. II., Pars II.

ance of the Roman *curia* in the municipalities of the Lombard kingdom. They seize upon a few names, relics of Roman rule, and from them generalize a complete system of taxation and administration. That the existence of any such system is alike contrary to fact and to the whole nature of the Lombard people, any critical and impartial study of the sources of government revenues at this time will make clear. It would be out of place to burden a paper of this character with the results of a minute investigation into the fiscal relations of the rulers and the people when this has no immediate connection with the development of municipal government; but I will state that a careful examination of all available sources, including documents and statutory enactments, both public and private, reveals, to my mind, a theory and a system of raising the revenues of the state closely allied in both principle and detail to feudal forms and feudal ideas, and having little in common save the names of a few of its officers, with the ancient methods of collecting the taxes peculiar to the Roman municipal constitution.[42]

In general terms, the collectors of the revenues were called *telonarii*, or *actores*, *exactores* or *actionarii*, etc., and the taxes they collected were the usual feudal dues, fines, forfeitures, compositions for service, etc. The nomenclature of these various officers and of the different duties they had to levy, varying as it did with regard to locality, and more especially with regard to time—the Franks introducing an entirely new set of names for institutions often identical in character to those displaced—presents an amount of confusion which, fortunately, it is not necessary

[42] In illustration of this fact I will cite the names of some of the various taxes, dues and privileges, mention of which is found in the old documents. The feudal character of these will be apparent to the reader. Following the rough division indicated in the text, we have:

I. Under heading *"Fines and Forfeitures"*:

1. Forfaturae:

Forisfacturae,
Multae (Mulcte),
Freda,

e.g. Leudis (Leudum) for homicide.
Penalties and compositions for crime.

2. Scadentiae:

Excadentia,
Bona caduca.

Publicum falls heir to various classes of individuals. Cf. Leg. *Rhotari*, No. 158 et al.

3. Lagan (Laganum).

Seizure of shipwrecked goods by the state. Examples more common after year 1000 A. D.

II. Under the head of *"Taxes and Privileges"*:

1. *Onera Publica*, or Angariae (Perangariae), Factiones publicae.

a. Heribannum: Penalty for avoidance of military service. Cf. *Charlemagne*, Leges, No. 23 et al.

b. Heribergum: Hospitality to *Missi* of emperor or king. Cf. *Charlemagne*, Leges, No. 128 et al.

c. Mansionaticum (Mansiones, Evectio): Lodging for king and his ministers.

Conjectum was a pro rata tax on a district so as to meet the expense. Cf. *Lud. Pius*, Leg. Nos. 54, 24, et al. loc.

Tractoria gave specification of what should be provided in each case. For Formula, v. *Marcolfo*, Lib. I.

d. Veredi (Paraveredi): Horses and beasts of burden for king and ministers. Cf. in Capitular. Reg. Franc. saepe. Capit. *Lud.* II., Ad Missos, etc.

Census vehicularius, fiscalis or publicus was post to carry, free of expense, king's letters, etc.

e. Foderum (Fodrum): Support of a king and his army in passing through a district. Cf. many privileges and exemptions to different churches and monasteries. Articles of the Peace of Constance. Some privileges to private persons.

2. *Teloneum.*

a. Pedagium: General word for *tolls* on streets, roads, bridges, etc.

α. Pontaticum, for bridges.
β. Portaticum, for gates.
γ. Platiaticum, for license to sell in market.
δ. Casaticum, for houses.

Cf. *Otho* II., Diploma to Monast. Volturno a. 983, et al. loc.

b. Ripaticum: General word for tolls and taxes for transport by water. Cf. Diploma of Berenger II. v. *Ughelli*, Italia Sacra, Tom. V. Also a Privilegium of Charlemagne, anno 787. v. *Ughelli*, Italia Sacra, Tom. V., a. 787. This privilegium confirms the laws of Liutprand, and shows how much the inhabitants of Como had to pay in various places in moving salt down the rivers of Lombardy.

α. Paliscitura,
β. Trasitura,
γ. Navium ligatura.

Wharfage dues.

δ. Portonaticum, harbor dues.
ε. Curatura, probably a tax on certain merchandise.
ζ. Passagio, probably same as preceding, but possibly a tax in favor of those going to the Holy Land.

3. *Auxilia* (Occasiones) (dues from vassals):

a. Praestitiones.
b. Dona.
c. Gratuita.
d. Mutua.

More common after the year 1000 A.D.; but, for an example in the year 878, see a Diploma of Lewis II., published by *Puricelli* in his Monumenti della Basilica Arnbrosiana.

for us to endeavor to penetrate; but, having stated the foregoing general conviction with regard to the fiscal system, we will now pass on to a consideration of some of the lesser offices held within each *civitas* by the deputies and subordinates of the *dux*. These, of course, were connected, in degrees more or less close, with the different *curtes regiae*, and with the *placita* held in the various *civitates* commonly about three times in the year. Some of the officers, like the *vice-comes* found to have existed in many localities, are simply deputies of the *dux*, or representatives of his person, and hold their office simply by virtue of his will and under a somewhat arbitrary tenure; others, like the gastald, the *sculdahis*, and later the *scabinus*, represent offices which formed an integral part of the constitution of the government, and appointment to which, whether made by the *dux* or by the central power, involved a necessary duty of a determinate character. An accurate determination of the relative positions of these various minor officials, of the extent of their jurisdiction and of its limitations, presents one of the most difficult problems which the student of these dark ages of history is called upon to solve. The peculiar character of the sources from which we have to derive all our information makes it quite possible for all writers on the subject to disagree with regard to details, and leaves a wide margin for discussion even on the important characteristics of the various offices. Avoiding as much as possible the points of controversy, I will endeavor to give the general features of the more important of these offices, the conclusions given in each case resulting from an examination of the different theories held and of the sources on which these are based.

The officer who seems to have ranked next in importance to the *dux* within the limits of the *civitas* is the gastald, who goes indifferently by the name of *gastaldus, castaldius,* or *gastaldio.* His powers were of a judicial character, and he shared with the *dux* the title of *judex;* but whether he enjoyed the full prerogative of a *judex civitatis,* or whether his judicial functions were of a more limited character and referred exclusively to matters of a fiscal nature belonging to the *curtis regia*

III. Under head of *"lands owned by Crown or Publicum"*:

1. *Terra Censualis.* Holder of t.c. owed these duties:

    a. Glaudaticum,
    b. Escaticum,
    c. Herbaticum,
    d. Datio,
    e. Alpaticum,
    f. Agrarium.

    Payments for right to pasture cattle and swine on public lands. Cf. Chron. da Volturno, a. 972. Chron. Farfensis. Privileg. Lud. Pii, et al. loc.

    g. Terraticum, amount of produce given for right to cultivate.
    h. Pascuarium, payment for sheep pastured on the public land.
    i. Boazia, tax levied on every pair of oxen; probably not developed before XII. century.

The taxes and so forth mentioned in this list are by no means all that were levied, but are a fair representation of them. After the year 1000 their feudal character is even more strongly marked.

or the *camera* of the king, is a question to which the evidence to be gathered from the law codes gives no decided answer.[43] It seems probable, however, from the importance seemingly attached to the holders of this title in the many cases in which they are mentioned in the old laws and documents, that their jurisdiction was of a broader character than would be implied by a restriction to purely fiscal functions; in fact, that it approached more nearly to the power of the *dux* and *judex civitatis*, though being in some way of less extent or possibly supplementary to it. Perhaps the distinction would come out more clearly if we said that the office was characterized by its relations to the fiscal functions of the state, but that its duties and privileges appear not to have been restricted to affairs of that nature. It is certainly true that very many instances occur in which the duke and the gastald are alluded to, whether in laws or in contracts, in precisely the same terms and in positions which would seem to indicate an almost perfect equality of dignity. As, for example, in a meeting between Liutprand and Pope Zacharias, described by Anastasius Bibliotecharius,[44] where dukes and gastalds are together reckoned among the *judices*: here the king goes to meet the pope "cum suis judicibus," and gives him as an escort "Agripandum ducem Clusinum, nepotem suum, seu Tacipertum Castaldium et Remingum, Castaldum Tuscanensem." In spite of this apparent equality, however, it seems to me nearer the truth to consider the position of the gastald as an inferior one to that of the *dux*, especially in Lombard times, before that official was replaced by the *comes* of the Carlovingians.

The important point which it is necessary to emphasize in this connection is the fact that the gastald held his tenure, not from the *dux* as his subordinate, but from the king in person, and for this reason can more fitly be compared with the later count than with the *dux* of the Lombards. Consequently it is in the matter of tenure that I think is to be found the difference in power between the two officers. In addition to his official authority, the *dux* was possessed of a power and an influence entirely his own, derived quite as much from the number of his vassals and his position in the *civitas* as from the grant he received from the king. At home he was a powerful lord, and though he, of course, owed fealty and service to the king, he was by no means a king's servant, like his successor the Carlovingian count. The gastald, on the other hand, was eminently a servant of the central power; and whether or not he was engaged exclusively in looking after the fiscal interests of

---

[43] This statement, while true of all integral parts of the Lombard kingdom, must, however, be modified in regard to the great duchies of Spoleto and Beneventum, which were under a different system of internal government from the kingdom of Lombardy proper—were, in fact, small tributary kingdoms under great dukes enjoying practically royal powers. The Duchy of Beneventum seems to have been divided into *gastaldata*, divisions of territory similar to the *civitates* of Lombardy, but presided over by a gastald instead of by a *dux* or *comes*. In the charter of division made between the dukes of Beneventum and of Salerno in the year 851—v. *Muratori*, Ant. Ital. Diss. X.—are mentioned "integra gastaldata, seu ministeria Tarentum, Latinianum, Cusentia, etc." And, at an earlier date, *Paulus Diaconus*—De Gest. Long., Lib. V., cap. 29—tells of a certain "Alzeconis Dux de Bulgaris," to whom Grimoald, Duke of Beneventum, gives "ad habitandum ... Lepianum, Bovianum et Inferniam, et aliis cum suis territoriis civitates; ipsumque Alzeconem mutato dignitatis nomine, de duce gastaldium vocari praecepit."

[44] v. *Muratori*: Script. Rer. Ital., Tom. III., Pars II., p. 162D.

the masters who employed him, he had no power and no influence except such as he derived from the source of his authority. He was a king's minister and nothing more, and we can easily appreciate that the amount of power he was enabled to exercise could never exceed the amount of influence in local affairs possessed at any particular time by the central government, whose representative he was.

But the very nature of the source from which the power of his office is derived is what connects it vitally with the subject of our enquiry. We have seen the *dux* as head—in the earliest times almost independent head—of the whole *civitas*, including rural and city jurisdiction. We have seen him as an official, depending from the king, it is true, and holding the king's *placita* and executing the law, but also holding *placita* of his own; appearing as a powerful local lord, and exercising almost arbitrary power in the regulation and the distribution of the public property of the commonwealth over which he ruled; in fact, a descendant of the old *duces* of the Lombard barbarian host, who, perhaps, even antedating the royal office, held their power and their position as princes and chosen leaders of the people, rather than as appointees or dependents of any higher authority. In the gastald, on the other hand, we have an official of an entirely different type—one not belonging to a powerful class of lords or leaders which traces its origin to the spontaneous choice of the people or army, but one who gets his appointment at the will and in the interests of the central government, and is commissioned to exercise certain functions of the administration as an assistant to, perhaps even as a check on, the power of the local head.

Such an official was naturally located at the place where the district courts held their sessions, and where the fiscal duties which he especially had in charge were most easily executed. As we have seen in the case of the *dux*, convenience points to the *urbs* of each *civitas* as a natural centre, and consequently here again we find the office of gastald as another agent in bringing the municipal division into prominence; but doing this, we must always remember, simply from the fact of convenience or fitness, and not in any sense as a matter of constitutional necessity. Like that of the *dux*, the jurisdiction of the gastald was exercised over the remotest farm of the *civitas* as much as over the palace in the city: *de jure*, the city gained nothing by the circumstance of its being the centre of the administration of any office; but, *de facto*, the holding of such a position can easily be seen to have been an important element in its growth and development.

This fact is even of greater importance in the case of the gastald than in that of the *dux*, because, on account of the elimination of the character of local ruler, which was indissolubly attached to the office of the latter, the gastald brought local affairs into direct relation with other parts of the social system of the kingdom, especially connecting them with the king or centre of the whole. Such a connection, as may be inferred from what has just been said, while legally true, of course, of the whole *civitas*, had practically the effect of bringing the cities chiefly into relation with the rest of the Lombard constitution; and, consequently, some writers point to the office of gastald as the connecting link between municipal life and the new state life of the Teutonic system. This statement seems to me to be true except in so far as it makes the gastald the only connecting link. For we have already seen the *dux* holding the same relation, only in a less direct manner, owing to the intrusion of other interests belonging to his position; and we shall shortly have to consider the *scabinus*, another local officer, who, under Carlovingian rule, accomplished even more in this direction than the gastald. I do not wish to fail in appreciation of the important influence of this office in the development of the slowly growing idea of individuality in the cities of Lombardy, only to point out that it was not the only "connecting link" between the municipal units and the state as a whole.

In passing to a brief characterization of a few of the subordinate officers, I must not omit to mention the fact that the gastald had also certain military functions attached to his office. When called upon by the king he took command in the army, together with the minor officers who were under him in his jurisdiction, such as the *sculdahis, saltarius,*[45] etc. We have confirmation of this in the constitution "promotionis exercitus" of Lewis II.,[46] which says "ut nullum ab expeditione aut Comes aut Gastald, vel Ministri eorum excusatum habeant"; and in the life of Gregory II., Anastasius Bibliotecharius[47] tells that at the overthrow of the *castrum* of Cumae with the help of that pope, "Langobardos pene trecentos cum eorum Gastaldione interfecerunt." In military affairs the command held by the gastald seems to have been lower than that of the *dux*, the leader of all the troops furnished by the *civitas*. A right of appeal to the *dux* existed for the *exercitalis* who was oppressed by the gastald, as shown by the twenty-fourth law of Rhotaris,[48] which says: "Si Gastaldius exercitalem suum contra rationem molestaverit, *Dux* eum soletur." In a case of oppression by the *dux*, the gastald, on the other hand, could bring the matter before the king.

Before considering the changes introduced by the Carlovingian rule, let us cast a hasty glance at a few of the minor officers who acted as subordinates of the *judex* in administering the affairs of the *civitas*. As their relations to the urban portion of the Lombard kingdom, which is the special object of our study, were either slight in themselves or else so closely connected with those of their superiors as not to merit any particular description, I will merely mention the names of a few of them and indicate their duties. The officer who came next in rank to the *judex*, and who, in a subordinate capacity, assisted him especially in administering the judicial affairs of the *civitas*, was in Lombard times called the *sculdahis*, and in Carlovingian times the *centenarius*. Under him were the *saltarius* and the *decanus*. The *sculdahis* acted as a local officer under the *judex*, having limited judicial, police and military powers. His jurisdiction was confined to the small fortified towns and villages of the *civitas*, where he administered justice and collected fines, forfeitures, etc., in much the same manner as did the *judex* in the largest town of the *civitas*; his judgments, however, were not final, but always subject to appeal to a higher authority: "Si vero talis causa fuerit, quod ipse Sculdahis minime deliberare possit, dirigat ambas partes ad judicem suum."[49] There were several *sculdahis* in one

---

[45] *Liutprandi*: Leg. Lib. VI., Leg. 29. v. *Muratori*: Script. Rer. Ital., Tom. I., Pars II.
[46] *Muratori*: Ant. Ital. Diss. X., Vol. I., P. I., p. 121.
[47] *Muratori*: Script. Rer. Ital., Tom. III., p. 155A.
[48] Ed. *Rhotari*: Leg. 23 and 24. v. *Muratori*: op. cit., Tom. I., Pars II.
[49] *Liutprandi*: Leg. Lib. IV., 7.

judiciaria, and cases were often tried before more than one,[50] though each of the smaller local units seems to have had such an officer. Paulus Diaconus[51] speaks of "elector loci illius, quem sculdahis lingua propria dicunt, vir nobilis," etc.

These rural divisions seem sometimes to have been called *sculdascia*, for we have a diploma of Berengar I., of the year 918, given to the monastery of Sta. Maria dell' Organo,[52] where is mentioned "pratum juris imperii nostri pertinens de Comitatu Veronensi, de Sculdascia videlicet, que Fluvium dicitur"; and in a document published by Ughelli,[53] in speaking of the bishops of Belluno, "Sculdascia Belluni" is used. In Frankish times the *centenarius* held the same position as the *sculdahis* of the Lombards: his jurisdiction was similarly limited to minor offences; all cases involving capital punishment, loss of liberty, or delivering of *res mancipii*, being handed over to the count's court according to the legislation of Charlemagne.[54] The *decani* and *saltarii* were subordinates of the *centenarii* and *sculdahis*. They both presided over smaller local divisions than the *sculdascia*, and acted as deputies. In the laws of Liutprand,[55] speaking of a runaway slave, we are told that "si in alia judiciaria inventus fuerit, tunc decanus aut saltarius, qui in loco ordinatus fuerit, comprehendere eum debeat et ad sculdahis suum perducat, et ipse sculdahis judici suo consignet." The *saltarius* seems to have been originally a sort of guardian of forests, "custos saltuum"[56] or "silvanus";[57] and the name of the *decanus*, like the Frankish *centenarius*, is a survival of the old decimal division of the army and people. These minor officers, as well as other subalterns of the *judex*, are often met with under the common name of *actionarii*, which includes also the different sorts of *exactores, adores, advocati*, and all the lesser officials of the *fiscus*.

In the course of this investigation I have already referred to, and in a certain measure characterized, the changes introduced into the Lombard system of government consequent on the kingdom being absorbed into the great empire of Charlemagne. I have said that, owing to the similarity of institutions between the Franks and the Lombards, the changes made consisted rather in differences in the manner of enforcing the control of the central power than in any alteration in the institutional life of the people, but that there were certain exceptions to this general rule, which, in their mode of operation, though not in the intention of their author, materially affected, indeed greatly accelerated, the growth of individual life among the cities. We must now consider the nature of these exceptions.

---

[50] *Liutprandi*, Leg. Lib. IV., 8, says: "Si homines de sub uno Judice, de duobus tamen Sculdahis causam habuerint, etc."

[51] *Paulus Diaconus*: De Gest. Lang., Lib. VI., 24.

[52] *Muratori*: Ant. Ital. Diss. X., Vol. I., Parte II., p. 116.

[53] *Ughelli*: Italia Sacra, Tom. V.

[54] *Caroli Magni*, Leg. Lomb. 36: "Ut nullus homo in Placito Centenarii neque ad mortem, neque ad libertatem suam amittendam, aut res reddendas vel mancipia judicetur. Sed ea omnium in praesentia Comitum, vel Missorum nostrorum, judicentur."

[55] *Liutprandi*: Leg. Lib. V., 15.

[56] Chronicon Fontanellense, Cap. I. v. *Muratori*: Ant. Ital. Diss. X., Vol. I., Parte I., p. 117.

[57] *Rachis*, a decree of—existing in the Monast. of Bobbio. v. *Muratori*: Aut. tal. Diss., Vol. I., Part I., p. 118 (Diss. X.).

Under the Lombard system we have seen the administrative unit of the state to be the *civitas*, with its administrative head, the *dux*, at different times enjoying a greater or less degree of independence from control of the central power. We have seen the *dux* lord as well as judge in his own jurisdiction, and standing as the successor of the military leader chosen by the people, instead of holding the position of king's servant; this place being more properly filled by the gastald, who cared for the fiscal interests of the central power, whose appointee he was. Such a form of government, it can be readily seen, left no room for any strong development of the principle of centralization, and no scope for the exercise of any decided power or even of general supervision by the central authority. The heads of the *civitates* were the king's *judices*, it is true, and assembled to assist him in judgments at his general *placita* in the March of each year; but they bear the character also of local lords of no mean importance, and in some cases possessed of no inconsiderable amount of power. Such a degree of individual influence—perhaps I should exaggerate if I called it individual independence—was, however, little suited to the idea of a universal centralized empire, which was the forming principle of the government of Charlemagne. While recognizing the necessity of retaining the fundamental institution of a division of the state into *civitates*, and of governing it by means of the heads of these divisions, he wished to eliminate from these officers all the characteristics of local magnates, and to reduce them to the more easily controlled position of servants, and dependents of the king. This object he accomplished most satisfactorily by changing the dukes or local lords into counts or king's men, by appointing a Count of the Palace for Italy, and by extending to that kingdom the perfectly organized system of central control by means of the *Missi Dominici*, with the workings of which in the other parts of his great empire the student of history is too well acquainted to need any description here.

The immediate changes in the life of the people consequent on the introduction of this system were not considerable, if we except a great improvement in public order and a marked advance in the equitable administration of justice; but it needs no great foresight to see that the ultimate effects on the position held by the municipal units in the community could not fail to be important and far-reaching. The new officer, the count, stripped of all the importance that his predecessor, the duke, had enjoyed as lord of the country over which he ruled, was placed in each city to govern, in the king's name, it and its *territorium*. As long as the empire of Charlemagne retained its integrity, and as long as the reins of central government were held by a strong hand and the control it exercised was felt to be positive and real, the change in the character of the local governor was of little moment; but as soon as the power of the central government weakened—during the inglorious reigns of the immediate successors of the great emperor—its hold on the administration of the local units slackened immediately; and in proportion as the vitality of the new central control diminishes, we see appearing the effects which must always result when the strong hand of an active central power is removed from a system of administration which had been based on the exercise of such a power. These effects are the increased importance—I may now say the increased independence—of the local units; of these local units themselves as distinguished from the heads who rule over them.

The change had made these units more organic parts of the state than they had ever been before: we have seen them first made prominent by being the seats of the rulers of the *civitas*, and now we are to see them gain a more significant advance by coming into relation with the head of the state directly, instead of through the personal power of their lord. For the local ruler has yielded his individual pre-eminence to the central government; and when this fails to maintain its authority, in any community whose inhabitants are capable of fostering the seeds of independence once sown, it is difficult if not impossible for a successor to repossess himself of the privileges which have been forfeited. In any state where the seat of central authority is distant or its power only exercised feebly and at intervals, the local units secure much greater independence and importance, through the very necessity of performing many functions left unheeded by the ruler of all; and if the people are self-reliant in character, they will in time develop a sort of self-government which, although it would not at first think of questioning the theoretical right and overlordship of the central power, will eventually brook but little interference with its modes of procedure and with its exercise of functions, which the lapse of time has transformed from enforced duties into jealously guarded privileges.

This is the keynote of the later history of the Italian cities. This it was, and not any real lack of patriotism, which made them choose a German emperor instead of an Italian king. There was no room at that time for the idea of Italian unity, as we now understand it: the nature of the people alone would have rendered such a thing impossible, even if we leave out of account the fact that Italy was the meeting-ground of the two great powers of the mediaeval world, the Pope and the Emperor. Italy then must have had two masters, or have been the slave of one. The same spirit of civic independence which caused the development of Ancient Greece by preventing the universal rule of one power, caused the Italians, under different conditions, to pit one master against another to attain the same end. Even Liutprand, the old historian of the tenth century, recognized this. In the first book of his "Historia" he says: "The Italians wish always to serve two masters, in order to restrain one by means of the terror with which the other inspires him."[58] By means of holding in their hands the balance of power they hoped to rule their rulers; and to attain this object was the only reason which ever prompted the cities to unite with any degree of harmony. Local independence was what they aimed at, and their shrewdness showed them the only possible means in that age of securing it.

These results could hardly have been attained if society had remained such that the prominence of the local divisions was dependent on the prominence of the respective heads of these divisions; but the character of their local rulers once changed, and their powers in a great measure absorbed by the act of a strong central power, when that power fell to pieces it was much easier for the local divisions, as such, to increase their independence, and to utilize the advance they had made, by means of their more direct relation to the central power, to gain a position which they would enjoy in spite of the efforts alike of that power and of their old rulers. Such a position would not be reached except by means of great strug-

[58] *Liutprandi Ticinensis*: Historia, Lib. I., cap. 10. v. *Muratori*: Script. Rer. Ital. II., p. 431. *Pertz*, Monum.; Script., Tom. III.

gles and by passing through a period of great disintegration and of fierce internal strife between opposing factions, such as in the history of the Italian communes is represented by the dark period between the fall of the last of the Carlovingians and the election of the first German emperor as king of Italy; but once attained, the character of the people who accomplished it would ensure its permanence, as long as they retained those principles of independence which had made them victorious in the struggle. After this short discussion, in which we have traced the ultimate effects of the action of Charlemagne in changing the dukes into counts, let us look at another feature in the field of city government introduced by him, the new office of the *scabinus* or city judge.

According to the theory of judicial procedure among the Teutonic nations, judgment in criminal cases was given in the open court or *placitum*, where, besides the regular judges, all or any of the freemen within its jurisdiction were supposed to concur in the judgment and sentence. How far this method of arriving at judicial decisions was carried out in practice depended largely on custom and other local influences, and consequently varied greatly in different countries and with different nations. I do not propose to enter into the discussion[59] of the existence of these "judicators"[60] in Lombardy in the eighth century, but will only say that it is certain that before the Frankish conquest there did not exist a class of men whose business it was to assist the judge in disposing of cases. If through ignorance of the law or for other reasons he was unable to come to a decision, "si vero talis causa fuit, quod ipse ... deliberare minime possit,"[61] he could call some of the freemen to assist him: "advocis [advocet] alios ... qui sciunt judicare,"[62] etc., but this seems, in later times at any rate, to have been a privilege to be used at discretion, and the persons summoned were not regularly appointed officers of the court. The Lombard codes are silent with regard to these indicators; but Savigny,[63] in his argument to prove their existence, claims that mention is made of them in two decisions of Liutprand of the years 715 and 716, and brings as additional evidence a *placitum* of 751[64] in which Lupo, duke of Spoleto, gives judgment "una cum judicibus nostris ... vel aliis pluribus astantibus," etc. It is of more importance for us, however, to determine the reasons for the introduction into Italy by Charlemagne of the new office of the *scabinus*, than to lose ourselves in a complicated discussion of the theoretical predecessors of these officers.

The introduction of this new feature into city government seems to have been the result of an attempt to correct certain abuses in the exercise of power by the

[59] The opposite sides of the question are ably presented by *Savigny*: Geschichte des Röm. Rechts, etc., Vol. I., p. 230 et seq. (trans.), and *Hegel*; Städteverfassung v. Italien, etc., I., page 470, note.

[60] It is difficult to find an English word which intelligently renders the various names for these freemen in their judicial capacity, used by the different nations, such as *arimanni, rachinburgi, boni homines*, etc. Most English writers make use of the German word *schöppen*. I have taken the rendering "judicators" from Edward Cathcart, the translator of the first volume of Savigny's Geschichte des Römischen Rechts im Mittelalter.

[61] *Liutprandi*: Leg. 25, Lib. IV., 7.

[62] *Rachis*: Leg. No. 11.

[63] *Savigny*: Geschichte, etc., Vol. I., p. 233, trans.

[64] Preserved in the Archives of Farfa. Published by: *Mabillon*: Annales Ord. S. Bene-

duke or head of the courts of the *civitas*. The duke had the right, as we know, to summon all the freemen in his jurisdiction to his *placita*, and to fine them according to the law if they failed to answer his summons. The fines collected in this manner formed a substantial part of the revenues of the *judex* imposing them, and consequently arose the abuse, which seems to have been a great cause of complaint in the eighth century, that the freemen were summoned to attend *placita* at frequent intervals during the year, when there was no business of any importance to transact, and when the sole object of the summons was to furnish an excuse for imposing the fine. An attempt to remedy this injustice was made when the number of *placita* which any one *judex* could hold during the year was limited by law to three,[65] and the dates for these definitely determined. But the abuse does not seem to have been satisfactorily corrected till the time when Charlemagne formally substituted for the body of the freemen, who in theory were supposed to attend the *placita* and assist in the judgments, a limited number of men who, as regularly constituted judges, either assisted the *judices* or made judgments of their own, as the case might be. These officers were the *scabini*, whose position we are now investigating.

All of the best authorities agree that no authentic allusion to the office in Italy is to be found prior to the establishment of Frankish rule. The word *scavinus* or *scabinus* sometimes occurs, but in every case the document containing it has been proved spurious on other grounds. For instance, Brunetti[66] publishes a donation of the bishop Speciosus of Florence, to the monastery of the cathedral, purporting to belong to the year 724, in which a certain "Alfuso scavino" is mentioned; but it has been proved that the monastery was only founded in the year 760, and though it may, at a later date, have received the donation, the significancy of the use of the term vanishes. The first authenticated use of the name of the new judge seems to be in a *placitum* of Charlemagne of the year 781.[67] In this the parties to a suit are mentioned as having already appeared before the "Comitem et suos Escapinios." Eight years later, in a *Praeceptum* of Charlemagne,[68] commission is given to the *comes* Tentmann "superque vicarios et Scabinos, quos sub se habet, diligenter inquirat."

Now that we have indicated the origin and noted the first appearance of the new officer, let us examine his position and his duties. I am much more willing to allow to the *scabinus* the title of "city officer," than to the *dux* or even the count. We have seen the latter as one of the important connecting links joining the city to the

---

dicti, Tom. II., p. 154. *Muratori*: Script. Rer. Ital., Tom. II., Pars II., p. 341.

[65] We have confirmation of this from a document of the early part of the ninth century, which says: "De Vicariis et Centenariis qui magis propter cupiditatem quam propter justitiam faciendam saepissime placita tenent, et exinde populum minus affligunt, ita teneatur … ut videlicet in anno tria solummodo generalia placita observent et nullos eos amplius placita observare compellat." From Worms Capitulary of *Lewis the Debonnair*, a. 829, c. 5. Also compare: Capit. V., anni 819, Art. 14. Capit., Lib. IV., c. 57. (*Baluzii*, 616 infr., 788 supr.) *Caroli Magni*, Leg. Long. 69. (*Canciani* I., 157.)

[66] *Brunetti*: Cod. Diplom. Toscan. Doc. No. 18.

[67] *Bouquet*: Rerum Ghillicarum et Francicarum Scriptores.

[68] *Baluzii*: Capit. Reg. Franc. a. 789, Tom. V., p. 746.

state, bringing the city into relationship with the constitution of the kingdom and making it a part of it; but we have been unwilling to call the count or *dux* the *legal* head of the city, as such, that is to allow him the title of the first city officer. But with the *scabinus* the case is different. His mode of appointment, and the character of the functions he performed, ally him with the city proper and with city people. His duties and his interests were more confined to the city than those of any of the other judges, and when he accompanies the count to the general *placita* of the king, he seems to go in the capacity of a representative of the city, and more in the character of a city magistrate than any officer we have yet considered. His duties were almost entirely of a judicial character, and his powers seem to have been as broad in their extent as those of the other judges. That he had the power of imposing capital punishment, and that the other officers of the law could not change but only execute his orders, appears from the following passage:[69] "postquam Scabini eum [latronem] adjudicaverint, non est licentia vel Vicarii ei vitam concedere." Muratori[70] maintains that he also had the right of holding certain *placita* of his own, and cites in proof two *placita* of Lucca of the years 847 and 856, where we find: "Dum nos in Dei nomine Ardo, Adelperto et Gherimundo Scabini adsedentes in lucho Civitate Lucana," etc.; and "dum resedisset Gisulfus Scabinus de Vico Laceses, per jussionem Bernardi Comiti ... ubi cum ipso aderat Ausprand et Audibert Scavinis." In the first of these there is no mention whatever of the count, and in the second "Gisulfus Scabinus" acts with his associate *scabini* "per jussionem Comiti." But even if we allow to the *scabini* the right of holding *placita*, these must have been of a lower grade than those of the counts or of the *missi regii*; for to the *mallum* of the latter an appeal was allowed from the judgment of the *scabini*, as we see from the law of Charlemagne,[71] which says that: "Si quis caussam judicatam repetere in mallo praesumserit ... a Scabinis, qui caussam ipsam prius judicaverint, accipiat." Generally speaking, however, it seems probable that their jurisdiction included all cases arising within the city limits, which could be dealt with in the regular *placita* of the counts, and which were not of sufficient importance to be referred to the king in person, his representative the Count of the Palace, or his delegates the *missi regii*.

When the count went up to the general yearly *placitum* of the king, as the representative of the *civitas*, according to the laws of Charlemagne he was to be accompanied by a certain number of the *scabini*; and these seem to have accompanied him not solely in the character of legal advisers, but also in a certain measure as representatives of the cities in which lay their jurisdiction: they are by no means what the exaggeration of Sismondi[72] calls "des magistrats populaires ... qui representaient la bourgeoisie"; but they certainly stood for the interests of the people, in a greater degree than any of the ruling powers we have as yet considered. Their number is variously stated in the laws of different kings, and their actual number seems seldom to have come up to the standard of legal requirement. Lewis the Pious requires twelve to accompany each count when summoned by the em-

[69] Capit. I., Art. 13, anni 813. v. *Baluzii*: Capit. Reg. Franc., Tom. I., p. 509.

[70] *Muratori*: Ant. Ital. Diss. X., Vol. I., Pars I., p. 115.

[71] *Caroli Magni*: Leg. Long. No. 92.

[72] *Sismondi*: Rep. Ital. du Moyen Age, Vol. I., p. 268.

peror: "veniat unusquisque Comes et adducat secum duodecim Scabinos";[73] but concedes that if so many could not be found in the city, their number should be filled out from the best citizens of the town: "de melioribus hominibus illius civitatis suppleat numerum duodenarium."[74] According to Charlemagne,[75] no one should come with the count to a king's *placitum* unless he had a case to present, "qui causam suam quaerit, exceptis scabinis septem, qui ad omnia Placita esse debent." And again: "Ut nullus ad placitum banniatur ... exceptis scabineis septem, qui ad omnia Placita praeesse debent";[76] and seven seems to have been the usual number expected, and their attendance was compulsory; though sometimes only two appear, and in a few cases none at all.

Of all matters relating to this office, the one which is of most interest to us, and the one which most clearly shows the difference which was designed to exist between it and that of the other judges, was the manner in which the office was obtained. In this procedure we can trace almost distinctly that the object of the central power which established it was to secure greater justice and greater freedom to the subjects who came under its jurisdiction. The fact was recognized by the new government that the power of the local heads was too great to suit the principle of universal central control, which was the keynote of Charlemagne's system of administration, and was exercised in too arbitrary a manner; and that some check was necessary to curb the spirit and limit the independence of these local lords of the soil and the city who had little consideration for their inferiors, and who might at any time become a source of danger to their superiors. Such a check was found, in regard to the central authority, in the *missi regii*, and in reference to the general public, in the *scabini* or city judges.

In the old Lombard constitution we have seen the gastald, chiefly, however, in the matter of judicial decisions, exercise a controlling influence on the arbitrary action of the duke; but as the power of the count varied from that of the duke, so that of the *scabinus* differs from that of the gastald, only perhaps in a greater degree. At the time when the count assumes the place of his predecessor the duke, the *scabinus* displaces the gastald, although he cannot be said to have assumed exactly the same position as the latter, nor to have filled it in precisely the same way. The *scabinus* did not have, of course, any direct limiting control over the actions of the count; for any such power in the hands of a body of lesser officers would have been alike contrary to the spirit of feudalism which characterized the age, and impossible to its forms; but being the principal judicial functionaries of the district, into their hands fell most of the cases which formerly went to the *placita* of the count; and while the wish of the great emperor, that even the meanest subject of the realm should receive impartial justice at their hands, might have failed in its effect, its fulfilment was made more sure by the method prescribed for the election of the officers whose duty it was to execute it.[77]

---

[73] Capit. II., anni 819, Art. 2. v. *Baluzii*: Capit. Reg. Franc., Tom. I., p. 605.

[74] Loc. cit. sup.

[75] *Caroli Magni*: Leg. Long. No. 116.

[76] *Caroli Magni*: Cap. Minora, anni 803, c. 20.

[77] "Adjutores Comitum, qui meliores, et veraciores inveniri possunt." *Lothar I.*: Leg. No. 49. v. *Muratori*: Ant. Ital. Diss. X., Vol. I., Parte I., p. 112.

In describing the method by which the *scabini* gained their office, I am in some doubt as to the proper terms to be employed. I have just made use of the word "election," but cannot let it stand without some qualification. It was not an election in the strict sense of the word as we now understand it, but it was as near an approach to a popular choice as was possible in the age in which it existed. The citizens of a municipality did not nominate and elect by their votes a popular magistrate, as some writers would have us believe; for such a proceeding would have been an anomaly in the eighth century under the rule of a Frankish emperor. But the people had a voice, and from the frequent mention of their intervention it would seem an important voice, in the selection of those who were to be their judges, and who were to assist in representing them in the royal assembly. The original appointments were made by some higher power, in most cases the *missi regii*, the direct representatives of the king; but these were made not arbitrarily, but always "cum totius populi consensu." This was the important point; it was so far a popular office that the free consent of the people was always necessary to make valid the appointment of any incumbent. According to the ideas and customs of the eighth century, such a method of procedure would represent a fairly popular election; for we know well that in the times of the greatest freedom, the Teutonic idea of a popular vote never went beyond the mere expression of assent or dissent by the assembled freemen. The initiative was always left to the king or chief who conducted the meeting, just as much as it was in the ancient assembly held on the classic plains of Troy. In a capitulary[78] of Charlemagne of the year 809 it is decreed: "ut Scabini boni et veraces cum Comite et populo elegantur et constituantur": and more specific directions are given by Lothar I. in the year 873, in case of a *scabinus* found to be an unjust judge. He says:[79] "ut Missi Nostri ubicumque malos scabinos invenerint ejiciant, et totius populi consensu in loco eorum bonos eligant." From this latter example we see that the *missi* had the power of dismissal "for cause," as well as of nomination. In fact, the king and his ministers, in the interests of impartial justice, kept constant watch on the acts and judgments of the *scabini*, and a law of Lothar I. tells us that "quicumque de Scabinis deprehensus fuerit propter munera, aut propter amicitam injuste judicare" should be sent up to the king to render an account of the manner in which he had fulfilled the duties of his office.

Such then were the duties, the privileges and the restrictions of the first magistrate to whom we could venture to ascribe any of the attributes of a popular judge: a representative of the people at the assembly of their ruler; a judge of their suits and of their misdoings at home, and a check on the arbitrary power of their lord and feudal superior,—we can readily appreciate that the existence of such an officer within the city must have exercised some influence in giving to its inhabitants a greater sense of security, and consequently of importance, even if we cannot claim that in the earliest stages of municipal development it gave birth to any definite ideas of personal freedom or of municipal independence. But it can easily be seen that it formed another and an important factor in that idea whose progress we

---

[78] *Caroli Magni*: Capit. I., anni 809, Art. 22. v. *Baluzii*: Capit. Reg. Franc. I., 466 infr.

[79] *Lothar I.*: Capit. anni 873, Art. 9. v. *Baluzii*: Capit. Reg. Franc. Tom. II., p. 232. Leg. No. 48. v. *Muratori*: Diss. X., Vol. I., P. I., p. 112.

wish to trace, of a slowly growing feeling of individuality in the city as such, the municipal unit as conceived apart from the still legally recognized unit, the entire *civitas*. We have seen the count the representative of this idea as far as its actual connection with the constitution of the state was concerned, but it was the *scabinus* who was to represent it to the consciousness of the people, and to assist them in rediscovering the lost conception of a municipal unity.

It would be incomplete to conclude this account of the various officers of government, without some mention of the position held by the bishops at this period. As it has been our duty throughout this paper to study the municipalities of Italy as only preparing to assume a position of individuality eventually leading to independence, so it is with regard to the bishops. While their social influence, as pointed out in the first part of this paper, was always notable, their political power, which formed one of the important steps in the progress of the communes towards a separate existence, has its birth at a time which is beyond the limits of this investigation. Not until the overthrow of the Carlovingian dynasty left Italy the prey of contending factions, and the crown passing quickly from hand to hand made each applicant anxious to gain the support of the more prominent electors, did the bishops obtain that legally constituted political power which, by breaking up and in many cases destroying the rule of the counts and great nobles in the cities, was the means of bridging over the wide gulf which lay between the idea of a district under the almost absolute rule of a great lord, and a civic autonomy governed by its own independent citizens. Even, however, if we are not yet to portray the bishop in a position of high political importance, we may briefly consider his social power and influence, and, as we have done with the cities themselves, indicate the steps by which he was enabled ultimately to gain such an exalted position.

The relations of the bishop to the inhabitants of the cities during the period we are considering were pretty nearly such as described in the first part of this paper. He stood forth as protector of the weak and the oppressed; as mediator between an unfortunate prisoner and an unjust judge who was seeking his private interest rather than following the spirit of impartial justice; or between a downtrodden vassal and the almost unlimited power of his feudal superior. He lessened the severity of harsh judgments, he protested the imposition of unjust fines and penalties. In very many cases he was even appointed by the king or his representatives as co-judge to assist the *judex* or the *missus* in hearing cases where oppression or injustice was to be feared. But it is important for us to avoid confusing this kind of jurisdiction with that which he enjoyed in the century after he had attained the power and the office of count, and had combined the religious functions of head of the diocese with the secular ones of political ruler of the city. Any judicial authority possessed by the bishop at this earlier period was not in virtue of any political position he himself held, but came to him entirely in what might be called an extraordinary manner, that is, by delegation from the king, for definite specified occasions. As an example of this extraordinary delegated jurisdiction, I will refer to a document in the Archivio of the Canons of Arezzo[80] of the year 833, relating to the judgment of a dispute between "Petrum Episcopum Arretinum et Vigili-

---

[80] *Muratori*: Ant. Ital. Diss. LXXVII., Tom. III., Parte II., p. 189.

um Abatem Monasterii Sancti Antemi," situated in the territory of Chiusi, over a privilege ceded to that monastery by Lewis the Pious in 813.[81] The bishop of Arezzo gained a favorable decision from a court constituted of some *judices*, *missi* of the emperor, and of the bishops of Florence, Volterra and Siena, Agiprandus, Petrus and Anastasius. According to the terms of the document with regard to the composition of this court, the bishops sitting in it were "directi a Hlotario magno Imperatore"; and their powers are several times referred to as being "juxta jussionem et Indiculum Domni Imperatoris." Here, as in all other similar cases, we see plainly that there is no indication of any purely personal jurisdiction.

That the influence of the bishop in affairs of state at this period was only of an individual, extra-official character can be seen also from the fact that the king considered the bishops themselves to be under his judicial jurisdiction in all secular matters, just as the lesser clergy came under the jurisdiction of the *judices*:[82] and further, that after the election to a church, the decision of the *judex* must confirm the choice of the community in order to render it valid.[83] All disputes also between bishops and their clergy, between members of the body of clergy, and between these and members of the laity, were settled by the royal authority;[84] and what is most significant, there was a universal and freely used right of appeal for the clergy or laity from the decision of a bishop to the person of the king, who seems to have exhibited no hesitation in modifying or reversing sentences, even in matters relating to purely clerical discipline.[85]

Even in the time of the Franks, when the consideration shown to the church and its representatives was much greater than under any of the Lombard kings, we find Charlemagne,[86] on suspicion of infidelity to his government, having sent to him and retaining as prisoners the bishops "Civitatis Pisanae seu Lencanae" and Pottoni, Abbot of the monastery of Volturno; and Lewis the Pious[87] sends into exile "Ermoldo Nigello Abatis," and in the year 818 several other bishops, including Anselmus "Mediolanensis Archiepiscopus," "Wolfoldus Cremonensis" and "Theodolphus Amelianensis."[88] None of these restrictions and limitations, however, although they arose chiefly from the strong opposition always existing

---

[81] Vid. *Tommasio*: Historia sanese, Lib. IV.; *Ughelli*: Italia Sacra, Tom. III., for this privilege.

[82] *Brunetti*: Cod. Diplom. Toscan. No. 8, a. 715. A priest named Gunthram says: "Nec cumquam ab episcopum Senensem coridicionem habuimus, nisi, si de seculares causas nobis oppressio fiebat, veniebamus ad judicem Senensem, eo quod in ejus territorio sedebamus."

[83] *Brunetti*: Cod. Diplom. Toscan. No, 8, a. 715. Germanus, a deacon, says: "Quoniam prelectus a plebe, cum epistola Warnefried [the Gastald of Siena] rogaturus ambulavi ad Luperceanum Aretine Ecclesie Episcopum et per eum consecratus sum."

[84] For example see a judgment of the year 771, in the Archivio of Lucca. For which vid. *Muratori*: Ant. Ital. Diss. LXX., Tom. III., P. II., p. 184.

[85] Good illustrations of all these statements are to be found in two documents in the Archivio Archivescovile of Lucca, of about the year 813. Vid. *Muratori*: Ant. Ital. Diss. LXX., Tom. III., Parte II., p. 184.

[86] Codex Carolinus—*Adriani I.*, Epist. Nos. LV., LXXIX., LXXII., L.

[87] *Ermoldi Nigelli*: Poema. V. *Muratori*: Script. Rer. Ital., Tom. II., Pars II.

[88] *Muratori*: Ant. Ital. Diss, LXX., Vol. III., Parte II., p. 188.

between the local temporal rulers of the people and their spiritual rulers, could hinder the bishops from occupying that important position of mediators and of protectors of the people which we have ascribed to them.

Turning now to a consideration of the earliest steps which may be said to have cleared the way for the political power of the bishops, we are met by a subject which, though of great interest in itself, is not sufficiently a part of this investigation for us to do more than indicate the lines of its progress. This subject is the development of the practice of giving certain immunities and privileges to churches and monasteries, adopted by the Frankish kings, faithful sons of the church, and then followed by all their royal and imperial successors. In considering the important influence exercised by these immunities on the development of the espiscopal power and the effects of this on the growth of the communes, there are two essential facts which we must always keep prominently in mind. In the first place we must remember that the granting of immunities was a question of privilege to particular individuals or ecclesiastical institutions, and not a universal grant which affected in an equal degree all the dioceses of the realm. This led to the marked differences in rank and importance which existed between the various bishoprics, and in the tenth century, when the temporal power became in many cases an adjunct to the spiritual, caused some bishops to become powerful temporal princes, while others, unable to gain this pre-eminence, remained simply spiritual heads of their respective dioceses. So in the contest between the counts and the bishops we find the latter only victorious in certain cases, and consequently having only certain of the cities under their jurisdiction; a fact which is illustrated as late as the Peace of Constance, where in the ninth article the cities are still divided into episcopal and non-episcopal cities.[89] In the second place we must keep clearly before us an important fact, the truth of which any chronological account of the development of the principle of immunity would easily demonstrate, namely, that with the advance of time and with the growth of that principle, the changes which took place in the different sorts of immunities were not simply those of degree, but essentially and principally those of *kind*.

A descendant of Charlemagne may have granted to some monastery or bishopric a greater alleviation of some of the fiscal burdens borne by it under his immediate predecessor, but a successor of Berenger when he granted a *privilegium* did not simply perform the negative benefit of alleviating burdens; he endowed the head of the bishopric—probably in return for some service he had received at his hands or expected to receive with the positive benefit of the political headship and possession of some city or district of a former count. I mean by this that the earlier immunities—and in these are included all given during the period we are discussing—were all of them what are termed simple or ordinary immunities; that is, those which deal with exemption—whether from burdens for which the receivers would otherwise be liable, or from jurisdiction to which they would otherwise have been subjected—of what may properly be called the private possessions of the churches concerned. They had nothing to do with the privileges of a later time, by which a power to exact burdens was granted and a positive jurisdiction

---

[89] *Pertz*: Monum. German., Tom. IV., p. 176.

over others allowed: that is, public functions bestowed rather than private rights conceded.

That a distinction of such a character was a difference of kind and not of degree is so plainly apparent that it is unnecessary to dwell longer upon it, and it only remains for us to consider briefly the chronology of some of the changes that took place. If we adhere strictly to the proper signification of the terms used, the development can be somewhat succinctly described by the simple enumeration of the three characteristic features of its progress, viz. *protection, exemption, privilege* that is jurisdiction or temporal power; and the three periods which are covered respectively by the prominence of these ideas can be roughly stated to be: for the first, the reigns of Charlemagne and his successors down to the time of Charles the Bald—including any indication of this idea which we may find during the reigns of the last rulers of the first Lombard kingdom; for the second, the reigns of Charles the Bald, Karloman, and Charles the Fat; and for the third, the full development of the episcopal power in the tenth century, down to the period of its final decline, and the rise of actual municipal government within the communes.

It is doubtful whether immunities of any importance were granted even by the latest kings of the Lombards, before the invasion of the Franks. Under the first Lombard monarchy the church held a very subordinate position with regard to the state, and if privileges were granted to any of its members, they had attached to them no greater meaning than the simple extension to them of the *mundibrium* of the king, such as was often allowed to private individuals; that is, they were simply grants of royal protection, and were not similar to the later grants which included both protection and privilege.[90]

With the advent of Frankish rule under Charlemagne, marked consideration immediately appears for the church and its representatives. Not alone is ample protection granted to many of the churches of the kingdom, but to it is added the important function of exemption. The greatest evil endured in those days by the ecclesiastical authorities was exactions levied on their property and oppression exercised on their dependents by the dukes and counts under whose jurisdiction lay the temporal possessions of the churches and monasteries. Consequently the aim of every bishop and of every abbot was to obtain for the possessions of his diocese or his convent an exemption more or less complete from the civil administration of the neighboring secular ruler. For a long time there was no thought in the mind of the bishop of gaining for himself the functions of temporal jurisdiction, but simply that the power of the count should be restrained with regard to church property, that is, that he should not be able to exercise his judicial control over lands belonging to the church, except by the express permission, "per licentia data," and with the concurrence of the bishop himself. This and nothing more is what is meant by

[90] It is true that *Muratori* (Script. Rer. Ital., Tom. I., Pars II., p. 192) publishes a diploma to the monastery of Novantulanum, near Modena, purporting to be by Aistulf and of the year 753; and (in Ant. Ital. Diss. LXXI., Vol. III., P. II., p. 256) another by Desiderius to the monastery of Santa Giulia di Brescia, which seems to grant exemption and protection if not privilege. But in the first the formula employed is so exactly similar to that of the later Frankish documents issued for the same purpose, as immediately to excite suspicion; and in the second, Muratori himself finds something radically wrong with the chronology.

all of the charters of exemption granted by the Carlovingian rulers, down to the time of Charles the Bald, when, as we shall presently see, a change was introduced.

It would be useless for me to cite examples of such charters, for their number is countless, and reference may be made to any of the great collections of mediaeval documents for confirmation of what has just been said; for during the reigns of the earlier Carlovingians, the strong reverence for the church and respect for its officers which characterized the Frankish nation from the beginning led to the extension of these privileges to much the greater number of the churches in the realm. Not all churches enjoyed such grants, and not all those accorded were of the same liberal character, but the number given and the amount of liberty to the church thereby bestowed was sufficient to give to the clergy that degree of importance which ultimately culminated in making them the great lords that we find them in the tenth century. To give an idea of the tenor of these documents, I will, however, quote a few lines from the earliest one that has come under my notice in Carlovingian times, namely a diploma of the year 782, issued to Geminiano II., bishop of Modena, and preserved in the archives of that city. Here we find that: "Nullus judex publicus ad causas audiendum, vel freda exigendum, seu mansiones aut paratas faciendum, nec fidejussiones tollendum neque hominibus ipsius episcopatus distringendum," etc. This is sufficient to show the character of exemption from secular jurisdiction.[91]

The next forward step in the advance of the bishops to temporal power was made probably about the time of Charles the Bald; though under his two immediate predecessors, Lothaire[92] and Lewis II.,[93] we already see indications of an extension of the quality of exemption to include freedom from the payment of all public dues and the bearing of all public burdens.[94] It was precisely the introduction of this element of exemption from public burdens which marked the change in the nature of the immunities granted from the time of Charles the Bald, down to the period when the element of jurisdiction and real temporal power was introduced under Guido and Berenger. Up to this time, the grounds on which similar charters had been sought had been protection from the oppression of the counts, and had resulted, as we have seen, in the granting of simple charters of protection which were of no very great significance. But now it is exemption from public burdens, etc., that is made prominent, in addition to a complete severance from all jurisdiction and control of the secular power of the *civitas* in which the bishop's see and domains are situated. That this concession also was sought by the

---

[91] An even better example can be found among Charlemagne's diplomas, by referring to one granted by him to the church of Reggio, and published by *Ughelli*: Italia Sacra, Tom. V., Appendice.

[92] See a charter given by Lothaire to Pietro, bishop of Arezzo in 843, the year of the Treaty of Verdun, v. *Muratori*: Ant. Ital. Diss. LXX., Vol. III., Parte II., p. 196.

[93] See a law of Lewis II. of 855, made in the Diet of Pavia. v. *Muratori*: Script. Rer. Ital., Tom I., P. II. (added to Leg. Lomb.).

[94] Certain "dona," however, supposed to be voluntary, were always excepted. See a diploma of Louis of the year 854 to the monastery of St. Gall in Germany, where it describes the usual "dona" for *all* monasteries as "Caballi duo cum scuteis et lanceis." v. *Muratori*: Ant. Ital. Diss. LXX., Vol. II., Part II., p. 204.

bishop on the plea of protection for his dependents from oppression and exaction, does not diminish its importance; for it is easy to see that the line which separates recognized right of protection from recognized right of jurisdiction is one easily effaced, and defense from the tyranny of a foreign power can with little difficulty be transformed into domination by the professed defender.

That this was the order of development consequent on these changes is proved by the temporal dominion gained by the bishops in the next century; and the steps of its growth marked by numerous immunities granted by Charles the Bald, Karloman[95] his successor, and Charles the Fat, the last of the Carlovingians in Italy. As a good example of the complete development of this advance gained by the bishops, I will mention a charter given by Charles the Fat to John, bishop of Arezzo, in the year 879, in which he confirms to him all the property and the rights of that see, and takes him under his protection, "sub immunitatis suae defensione": he then goes on to explain what this term meant, giving a full account of the extent to which a bishop's property was exempted from the jurisdiction of the *judex publicus*, and protected from the imposition of burdens and exactions.[96]

The next step in the growth of the episcopal power, and the most important of all, is the progress from exemption to privilege, to jurisdiction; and occurs after the return of the kingship of Italy to the hands of native kings.[97] It means the full development of the bishop into the temporal ruler, and as such belongs properly to the history of the tenth century, and consequently is beyond the limits of the present paper.

We have now considered individually and separately, in the course of their development, the different elements which, when combined and modified by the various changes described, contributed to form the solid foundation upon which the fabric of the future independent life of the cities was to be built. We have been dealing exclusively with institutions, and the manner in which their growth has been accomplished. For it is in the institutional life of a people, and in the change and development it undergoes, that are to be found those elements which form the basis for all future changes, whether simply in the form of its government or in the structure of its social system. If once a clear picture is gained of the structural parts which form the institutional framework of any particular development, and a truthful presentation of these forming principles is proved and established, a detailed account of the material expression of them is a matter of secondary importance.

I have not, in this paper, attempted to describe the actual condition of any particular municipality, or even presented a picture which could represent the material existence of the cities as a whole. Such a picture would only be a necessary part of a study of institutions when the city itself was the unit to be investigated, and not of one whose chief object is to prove that the city as such had no constitu-

---

[95] See a *privilegium* given by him in the year 877 to the nuns of the Posterla, Sta. Teodata at Pavia. v. *Ughelli*: Italia Sacra, Tom. V.

[96] *Muratori*: Ant. Ital. Diss. LXX., Vol. III., Parte II., pp. 196, 197.

[97] Probably the earliest of such privileges was one granted to the bishop of Modena by Guido in the year 892, and published by *Ughelli*: Italia Sacra, Tom. II., p. 98.

tional existence, but simply formed a part of another institutional unit. When we reach a period in which the city stands out as an object of study in itself, and when we do not have to trace its history only by learning that of other institutions which included and overshadowed it, then the practical life of the people within its walls becomes of the greatest importance, even to the smallest detail of civic law or city custom; and then, and not till then, begins what could properly be called a study of municipal institutions.

During the three centuries that we have been investigating, the study of the Italian municipalities has been, as we have seen, but the study of other institutions of which the municipality formed only a part. No attempt has been made to do more than prove the origin and trace the earliest development of those principles, which in their maturity were to gain for the municipal unit that position where the study of its own structure would become an object of interest, entirely apart and distinct from any of its surroundings. It has been shown that the city did not inherit any such position from its immediate predecessor the Roman *municipium*, which we have learnt to consider as overthrown, from a constitutional standpoint as annihilated; but that the new principle introduced into state life by the northern conquerors of Italy, the principle of administration by county rather than by urban divisions, relegated the city to an inferior place as part of a rural holding, instead of leaving it the centre of a circle of rural dependencies. Having demonstrated the absence of all constitutional recognition of the municipal unit as such, I have attempted to show how a condition of such legal insignificance became generally a condition of actual importance; how from a position of such negative interest, the advance of the city was commenced along a road which was ultimately to restore it its old pre-eminence, even adding to this in time the almost forgotten attribute of sovereignty. The motives for this advance we have seen to be no higher ones than convenience and expediency, which made the *urbs* of every *civitas* the natural centre of its local administration, thereby in fact, if in no way by law, restoring to it some of the elements of individuality, if not of pre-eminence, which it had lost. The means employed we have seen to be the functions of the various officers of state: the *dux*, the count and the gastald, who connected the city with the state, and the *scabinus* and the bishop, who represented this connection to the consciousness of the people. We have noted the marked effects produced on the development of a more popular feeling, by the changes introduced by the great emperor of the Franks; which, by diminishing the power of the local lords, accomplished a double benefit; on the one hand by saving the people from the arbitrary rule of a feudal superior; on the other, by causing the city to become more of a dependence and more of a support to the state as a whole. And finally we have left the city prepared, on the return of another dynasty of native kings, to accept, at least in a large number of cases, the domination of another kind of lord, a spiritual one; who was to serve as a medium for breaking up the power of the old lords of the *civitas*, and from whom it would be an easier task for the commune of the future to wrest the power and the sovereignty which was to make it a free and independent autonomy.

*   *   *   *   *

AUTHORITIES REFERRED TO IN THE TEXT AND FOOT-NOTES.

Anastasius Bibliothecarius: Vitae Romanorum Pontificum. v. *Muratori*: Script. Rer. Ital., Tom. III., Pars I.

Baluzii, Stephanus: Capitular. Regum Francorum additae sunt *Marculfi* Monachi et aliorum formulae veteres. Parisiis, 1780. 2 vols. fol.

Bethmann-Hollweg: Schrift über den Ursprung der lombardischen Städtefreiheit.

Bouquet, Martin: Recueil des historiens des Gaules et de la France, etc. Paris, 1738-1855. 21 vols. fol.

Brunetti: Codice Diplomatico Toscano. Firenze, 1806.

Canciani, Paolo: Barbarorum Leges Antiquae, etc. Venetiis, 1781-1792. (Formulae Baluzii, Marcolfi & Mabillon.)

Chronica Farfensis. v. *Muratori*: Script. Rer. Ital., Tom. II., Pars II.

Eichhorn: Deutsche Staats- und Rechtsgeschichte. Gött., 1803-23.

Fumagalli, Angelo: Codice Diplomatico S. Ambrosiano. Milano, 1805.

Hegel, Carl: Geschichte der Städteverfassung von Italien. Leipzig, 1847.

Leo, Heinrich: Verfassung der lombardischen Städte. 1820.

Liutprandus Ticinensis: Opera, v. *Pertz*, Monum.; Script., Tom. III.

Lex Salica. v. *Canciani*: Barbar. Leg. Antiq., Tom. V.

Lupo, Mario: Codex Diplomaticus civitatis et ecclesiae Bergomatis, etc. Bergomi, 1784-1799. Vols. 2.

Mabillon: De Re Diplomatica. Parisiis, 1709. (General Collection.) — Annales Ordinis S. Benedicti. Parisiis, 1703-39.

Macchiavelli, Nicolo: Istorie Florentine, *v.* Delle Opere, Tom. II., ed. Milano, 1804.

Migne: Patrologiae Cursus Completus, etc. Series Latina.

Muratori: Scriptores Rerum Italicarum. Mediolani, 1723. — Dissertazioni sopra le Antichità Italiane, etc. Roma, 1755.

Otto (Freising): Chron.

Pertz: Monumenta Germaniae Historica, etc. (Diplom.; Leges; Script.)

Paulus Diaconus: De Gestis Langobard. v. *Muratori*: Script. Rer. Ital., Tom. I.

Savigny: Geschichte des Romischen Rechts im Mittelalter, etc.

Sismondi: Histoire des Républiques Italiennes du Moyen Age. Paris, 1840.

Tacitus: Germania.

Tiraboschi, Girol: Storia della Badia di S. Silvestro di Nonantula, etc. Modena, 1784-1785.

Tomasini, Ludov.: Dei Benefizii.

Tommasio: Historia sanese.

Troya: Delia Condizione dei Romani, etc.

Ughelli: Italia Sacra. 10 vols. fol. Venetiis, 1717-1722.

Collections of documents in the *Archivii* of many cities of Northern Italy.

N.B.—The above list is restricted to those works to which direct reference is made in the text and foot-notes.

Lector House believes that a society develops through a two-fold approach of continuous learning and adaptation, which is derived from the study of classic literary works spread across the historic timeline of literature records. Therefore, we aim at reviving, repairing and redeveloping all those inaccessible or damaged but historically as well as culturally important literature across subjects so that the future generations may have an opportunity to study and learn from past works to embark upon a journey of creating a better future.

This book is a result of an effort made by Lector House towards making a contribution to the preservation and repair of original ancient works which might hold historical significance to the approach of continuous learning across subjects.

HAPPY READING & LEARNING!

LECTOR HOUSE LLP
E-MAIL: lectorpublishing@gmail.com